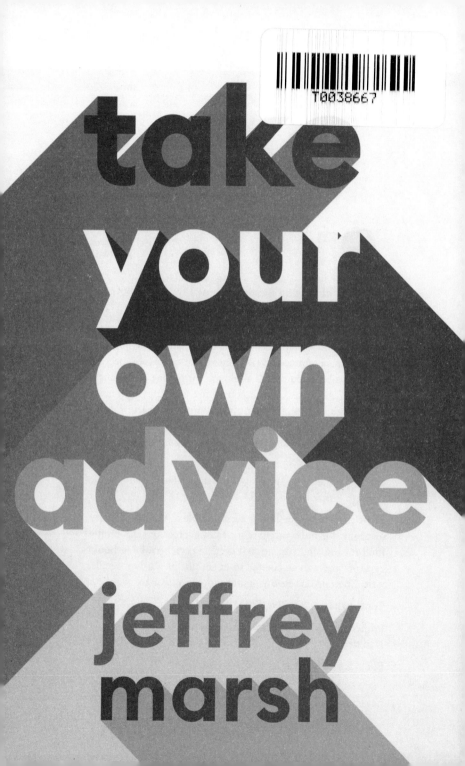

take
your
own
advice

jeffrey
marsh

an imprint of Penguin Random House LLC
penguinrandomhouse.com

Most TarcherPerigee books are available at special quantity
discounts for bulk purchase for sales promotions, premiums,
fund-raising, and educational needs. Special books or book
excerpts also can be created to fit specific needs. For details,
write SpecialMarkets@penguinrandomhouse.com.

Trade paperback ISBN: 9780593541173

Printed in the United States of America
1st Printing

Book design by Shannon Nicole Plunkett

take your own advice

Learn to Trust Your Inner Voice
and Start Helping *Yourself*

A TarcherPerigee Book

For Jeff, without whom I'd be quite lost.
You reflect back to me the best of who I am.
This book is for anyone who was told
they are "too much."

Contents

Introduction

Being "That Way"

I dreamed about you. I dreamed that one day we would meet. Growing up on a lonely farm in Pennsylvania, with only trees for friends, I often felt alone. And many times, I wished for a community and a new kind of family. I hoped for a family that would love me for who I am and accept every bit of me. And here you are. Here we are. On the farm, my family didn't get who I was. So, I would sneak into our barn and play dress-up— just to escape. As I twirled in that barn, what I imagined was a kind of audience. I imagined community and a celebration of life with many beautiful people. I imagined all of us together. And now my dream has come true, because you are here. But of course, when I imagined you in the barn, I also had one ear open for the sound of my dad's boots on the gravel outside the barn door. I was so afraid of that sound.

We lived down a long dirt road. The road went so far out into the country that we didn't even have an address. We had a mailbox at the end of our dirt driveway.

We lived at RD 60. We were part of the rural delivery system. And it felt for the longest time that we were also on the edge of the world. I thought there were no people like me. And at the time, there certainly didn't seem to be any people like me in that rural part of Pennsylvania, where the Klan would march down Main Street once a year for their perverse version of a pride parade. But I had friends in my imagination. I don't know how, but I knew about you before we met. I imagined you cheering me on.

I imagined a sense of belonging. It was a belonging that grew like a lotus out of the muck and grossness of my childhood. But in the world outside my imagination, I had to tell lies and hide. To straddle both worlds, I had to do many quick costume changes. I'd be in a dress; I'd be sparkling and dancing in the barn. I'd be having fun and laughing and twirling, then *crunch crunch*—my dad's tires, turning into our dirt and gravel driveway. Dad's tires sounded different from Mom's tires. And then, Dad's boots. I can still hear the heavy crunch of his tired footsteps. And I knew I was in trouble. And I knew that at least I would be in a *situation* if Dad saw me being myself, sparkling, feeling alive.

I can't remember my father ever uttering the word *Vietnam*. He was there, but never mentioned it. My father didn't talk about many things. Years later I would understand that the war in Vietnam became a sort of endless living nightmare for the men of my dad's generation. And many soldiers who came back from Vietnam returned to a world that was very different from the one they'd left. And maybe it didn't seem, didn't feel, like a return to real life. But I don't know. Dad never talked about it.

We especially didn't speak of my burgeoning non-binary soul. I don't think my parents had all the skills necessary to parent an LGBTQ child. And I think they lacked the skills needed to parent healthily, period. My parents used almost every tactic they could to try to get me not to be me. And that included withholding affection and manipulating, as well as many carrots and sticks. I also experienced violence.

At a very, very, *very* early age, I learned that if I was going to be me—if I was going to thrive, if I was going to dance, if I was going to have freedom—I would have to build a new life for myself. I would have to imagine new possibilities for myself. I would need to save myself. In our current world of TikTok, Instagram, and out and proud celebrities, it's hard to imagine a world where I felt I was the only one like me. But I can remember questioning if I was born on this earth, wondering if I had traveled here from a different planet, before *Will and Grace* was on TV, the first *Will and Grace*. Before *Queer Eye*, the first *Queer Eye*.

I felt all alone so often. My mom would eventually become a pastor, and I always felt like I was lying to God. When I was six, another kid from my church told me that God would never accept me. He said that if I didn't change the core of who I am, I was going to hell. And that *hell* was another word for "the ultimate separation from

God." So, I immediately started to memorize the Bible. I became the perfect Christian. My theory was that if I could remember every Bible verse, if I could have a favorite Bible verse ready for every occasion, if anyone suspected me of the very dark, evil, and awful stain of being LGBTQ, that person would immediately think, "Oh, no, not Jeffrey. Jeffrey's too good of a Christian, Jeffrey couldn't possibly be 'that way.'"

Well, it turns out I was very much "that way." And I learned that I could lie to the adults and the children around me. But of course, I felt like I could never lie to God. God sees everything. God saw me. But I feel like *you* saw me too—that when I was in the barn and twirling in my glittering skirts and being free, being me for the only time in my life, kicking up my heels, you were there. I like to joke with my very close friends that our inner children knew each other. Our inner children were friends when we were all growing up. And that's what it feels like in my imagination. I was surrounded by people clapping, laughing, having fun, hugging, and enjoying each other's presence. As a child, anyone was welcome to dance with me. I felt like I would've died for anyone to come into that barn and love me for who I was. I would have been delighted for anyone to wear a skirt with me (or whatever their version of a skirt was) and dance and have fun.

I almost died waiting for and wanting that kind of family. And here we are. That's why I never take for granted our relationship. I never take for granted the chance to speak to you. And I never take for granted the opportunity to tell you a little bit of my story, the things I've seen and the things I've learned along the way. I thought about *leaving* more than once. When I found Buddhism, I had some of the most joyous feelings of self-acceptance I have ever known. At one point, when I was living at a Buddhist monastery in California, I experienced intense feelings of despair, more intense than I have ever encountered in my life. Like any good spiritual path, my Buddhist training amplified and intensified all my feelings, sometimes all at once.

Your Light Will Always Balance Out Your Dark

I was preparing to return to the outside world at thirty years old at the end of a particularly extended stay at the monastery. It was three in the morning, and I was meant to leave the following afternoon. I was in a dark place. We, as Buddhist practitioners, stayed on the monastery property in little huts called hermitages. Hermitages are extremely rustic cabins in the woods, in this case near the beautiful Sierra Nevada. Each hermitage had a single glass lamp for lighting. Each had one chair on the porch to sit in and from which to look through the trees and see the sky. And I remember, as I was about to leave the monastery, that I couldn't sleep in the dark hours of the early morning. I walked onto my little porch among tall trees. I looked up at brittle stars. As I was watching the stars, I was observing my brain. My mind was telling me a story of how I shouldn't be here—not just that I shouldn't be here at the monastery, but I shouldn't be here in this life. It was a familiar story. There was one time when I was a teenager, Mom had come home, and I had attempted not to be here. I was being beaten up every day at school. I didn't think it was fair. I believed that if I lived in a world where I had to go to school every day and get beat up and made fun of and mocked, God was cruel. And that was a world I didn't want to be in anymore.

Mom called Poison Control. She found out that if I drank some milk, I would be just fine. She said almost nothing, but she did hug me. Then she sent me off to school the next day.

That time came flooding back to me at the monastery. I watched my brain go into the same ruts and patterns, like a wagon wheel on a worn country road. And I did something I've never really done before with those thoughts. I sat with them. The monastery kept a lamp lit in the meditation hall all night long. And if you were staying there or in residence at the monastery, you were welcome to use the meditation hall and meditate any time you liked. So, I left my little cabin in the woods and traveled along the winding dirt path that took me to the center of the monastery's property and the meditation hall.

I sat in the near darkness, watching the lamplight flickering on the wall with my legs crossed and my breath choppy. My heart rate was high, and my thoughts were spinning. Then, finally, I began to speak to myself. I don't remember when I got the idea or the inspiration, but it seemed fitting. "I'm not going anywhere. I'm with you. I'm glad you're here. Jeffrey, thank you for trying so hard. Thank you for who you are." At three in the morning, with a lamp flickering and my cross-legged shadow dancing on the wall, I committed myself to that voice. I made a vow to treat myself with the kindness I deserved and treat myself like the family I'd always wanted.

> **I made a vow to treat myself with the kindness I deserved.**

A Book for You, Born in the Light

That story reminds me of you. I don't know if that *needed* to happen. I don't know if I needed a direct experience of kindness and love before you came into my life, dear reader, but it certainly feels like a match. It feels like your kindness has resonance. The way I speak to myself is the way you see me. The next day at the monastery, the guide, the woman who runs the monastery property and is the religious teacher there, told me something I will never forget. She said, "You notice that there is no cliff on the monastery property. There is no lake here. When we begin to open our hearts, we start to discover what we truly deserve and begin to treat ourselves with kindness. When we make a commitment to ourselves, when we begin to open our hearts and find freedom, the feelings of self-doubt and despair will fight back."

I value you so much. Yes, you, reading this book. You are why I wanted to write *Take Your Own Advice* in the first place. I know you have a similar voice of kindness inside you that is just waiting to break free and tell you, "I love you. Thank you. I'm so glad you're here." You've heard that voice before. I bet you know how to act with kindness toward others. And I bet you might need some empathy, context, care, and encouragement from somebody who can embody that voice almost 24/7: you. I hope you realize you're a good person.

I don't think anybody would read this book unless they were kind. And honestly, in the world we live in that still wants to treat nonbinary people and LGBTQ people in general like poo-poo, you are making a different choice. You've already chosen kindness. You've already chosen life. You have already committed yourself to end hate in its many forms. The time has come to practice the wisdom you already know. The time has come to take your own advice.

You may not know me, but in my heart, we have met. We know each other well, which is how I know that you give the best advice. I know your friends turn to you. I know you sacrifice yourself for everyone else. This book is about how to get out of that habit. I want you to receive all you've been pouring into the hearts of others.

When I wrote my first book, *How to Be You*, I wanted everyone to enjoy the realization that they might not be such a bad person. I longed for readers to realize their ultimate worthiness. I wanted everyone to see themselves from outside of themselves for long enough to find kindness. I wanted people to be at least as kind to themselves as they would be to a stranger. *Take Your Own Advice* is an intentional follow-up. I had received thousands of emails from people who, when they shifted their self-perspective toward kindness using *How to Be You*, found wisdom. Self-hate and our ordinary judgments about ourselves obscure our natural, sparkling, inherent understanding. I had to write about that wisdom and "inner advice," and *Take Your Own Advice* was born.

I've identified the eight rules you'll need to follow to take your own advice. In my work as a Zen coach, bestselling author, and spiritual leader, I've found it essential that every person point their heart and mind toward *becoming their own coach* as quickly as possible. This book will help you do that. The road map we'll follow together is simple. Not necessarily easy, but simple:

Part 1 will give you excellent context and practical tips for strengthening your relationship with yourself. There is no spiritual growth until you understand that you are a good person who *deserves* spiritual growth.

Part 2 builds on part 1's self-acceptance foundation. This is your guide to changing your dynamic with other people. Once you have a strong relationship with yourself, you can consciously build the community you've always wanted. Therefore, you will love yourself and can be vulnerable with and love others with tremendous enthusiasm.

Part 3 is dedicated to the highest spiritual principles that transcend a sense of self versus other. You will learn to embody the spiritual principles of fearlessness. What is beyond self-kindness? What happens next? By the time you've reached the end of this book, you will see the value of your wisdom, and you will feel confident enough to trust yourself. Like many good adventures, your first assignment will be to accept yourself unconditionally.

Don't worry; it's not as hard as you think.

Part 1

Strengthen Your Relationship with Yourself

Have you ever considered dating yourself? Getting to know yourself? Spending quality time with yourself? Have you ever thought about committing to yourself for life? There are many reasons that we want to focus on other people making us happy. We want to love others and date others. We want to be liked and admired. But do you admire yourself? How much time do you spend working on liking yourself?

There's nothing wrong with caring about what other people think of you. Almost every human being does. But if your focus is always outward, you will constantly feel off-balance. Our culture awards confidence, but not self-care. It is a huge mistake to equate confidence with "not caring what they say." A truer definition for confidence may be "the ability to accept yourself in most situations."

It's easy for self-care gurus to say "be authentic" without warning people that authenticity can become an invisible standard. While you're trying to be authentic, you might have an unexamined assumption that you aren't doing it "right." It is much more important to build on your own experience of self-acceptance and concentrate on speaking your truth in each moment.

The answer is always self-kindness. The opposite of "I don't know what to do" is not always knowing what to do. The opposite of "I don't know" is a deep experience that you have your own back and that you love yourself no matter what happens. The answer you've always been looking for is the chance to do things you may be afraid to do, and to know you will respect yourself regardless of any outcome.

I would like to teach you how to achieve this level of self-acceptance.

Chapter 1

Stop Trying to Be Confident and Start Unconditionally Accepting Yourself

My Time with Tucker Carlson

The tweet was simple but surprising. It said, "I just saw @thejeffreymarsh on Fox News. The context [of the Fox News segment] was supposed to be 'liberals are so weird!' but it was honestly refreshing to see such a friendly face. . . ."

I was on my way home from the grocery store, and I had my reusable tote in my left hand, phone in my right, walking down the sidewalk and scrolling through Twitter. It was a sunny California day, and I felt free and easy. Then I saw the tweet, and I thought, *Oh no, my poor inbox.*

One of my TikToks had been featured on Fox News

a few months before. I got hate emails then. My video had played at around four o'clock Eastern time, and I don't know if that show was popular, so the hate messages had come and gone without a deluge. People who had seen Fox News reacted to the video, but it was nothing compared to what I assumed was about to happen.

From the tweet's timing, I knew that I had been in the A block on *Tucker Carlson Tonight*. On cable news, each show has four or five blocks. *Block* refers to the segments between commercials. The A block is first, D or E is last. And in general, they go in order of importance. If it bleeds, it leads, as they say. So, you put your most important, "sticky" material first. Producers of cable news put the most engaging material in the A block. That was me, I guess.

A Fox News producer had decided that one of my Tik-Toks was exciting. As a result, my TikTok played on Fox News during one of the most-watched moments of the week. Tucker Carlson's show, A block. At the very least, it was a viral time to be on TV, or should I call it "hate TV"? My inbox reflected the prime-time placement. Here's an example of an angry email I got; it's a direct quote: "STOP TARGETING YOUR F*CKING VIDEOS TOO KIDS LET KIDS BE KIDS YOU F*CKING F*GGOT."

Death threats filled my inbox over the next few days, and people on TikTok stitched my TikTok with their hate. A stitch occurs when a TikTok user takes an original TikTok and puts their video next to it—they can watch the original video and comment simultaneously.

She was watching my TikTok, sitting still, and simply loading a gun.

They then post their commentary on my video to their account. For example, a woman had made a video that got over 300,000 likes where she was watching my TikTok, sitting still, and simply loading a gun.

And like the TikTokers, Fox News viewers had reactions to my work! A reporter from *Rolling Stone* reached out to me and asked if she could interview me. I had posted some of the hate I was getting. And I had written about how that hate ballooned out of control. The reporter thought this was an essential milestone in the historic ways society demonizes LGBTQ people. And she also wanted to write about the general way that far-right extremists demonize people on the left.

My original TikTok *was* for kids. Here's a direct transcript:

"Hey, kids! It's possible to be like me and be happy. In fact, it's great to be like me and be happy. It's okay to like dresses, to like sparkly things. It's okay to be a little different than what people want you to be—than what people expect you to be. And (I'm old) and I grew up without any examples of people like me. And so I really, really wanted to tell you it's possible to be like me and then grow up and be happy. It's possible to be like me and grow up and be surrounded by wonderful friends, to be really, really fulfilled in your life, to have a good, long, happy life, and to . . . yeah, be joyful."

To me, telling kids that they should be themselves and that they have the right to be happy doesn't seem like a controversial message. But Fox News, now for the second time, thought my statement was controversial enough to feature my TikTok on air. So, my delightful and sexy and kind husband, Jeff, and I had to have a deep discussion. I remember going to him, a little afraid of what he might say, and he ended up telling me something that would change my life forever. It was one of the most profound things anyone had ever said to me. The conversation was about death—specifically, mine. If my inbox was filling with death threats, if my work was causing Fox News to demonize my life, soul, creativity, and nonbinary people in general, was it worth it? To the extent that I was in danger, I wanted his opinion about what we should do next. He surprised me a little bit by saying, "Make another video . . . Make *more* videos." As I'm typing this out on my computer, my eyes are starting to get a little teary because of his love for me.

Jeff continued, "Your mission is too important. Your path in life is too valid to change. I want to keep you safe, and I love you very much. I want to support you through the stress that these death threats cause so that you can deliver your strong, beautiful message to even more people." It broke my heart and filled my heart at the same time. I could barely take in how he could reflect unconditional love to me in such a dark situation. I'm not afraid to admit that I was deeply unsure of what

I should do at that moment. There have been many times throughout my whole career when I've been on the brink of deciding to pivot.

That day, Jeff's love kept me on track. But those beautiful words weren't the most important, profound thing he said to me that day. And that wasn't the part of our conversation that lives in my heart today. That wasn't the part that reverberates in my mind with crystal-clear memory. I had started our chat because I was under so much stress. I began to talk about how I might change my videos to make myself *safer*. How could I shift things? How could I word things differently? Should I change what I wear? Make myself less "LGBTQ looking"? What could I do about myself and my presentation or the words in my captions to make it less likely that extremists and hateful people would attack me?

You may have seen it coming. Jeff looked at me, his eyes crinkling with a smile. He said, "Don't you think . . ." (I love whenever he says "Don't you think" to me.) "Don't you think that they will use your words against you, take your words out of context, and use your words for their agenda no matter what you say?" Of course, he was right. And it's a crucial question. So, here I was at another crossroads, getting a life lesson in what it means to cling to what other people think of you. I was getting the "spiritual studies class" about trying to control the narrative of what other people think of me. It was prime time! On national television! People talked about how I am some monster—about how I am a danger to children. The Mister Rogers image I was going for shattered dramatically.

If you were traumatized as a child, one of the hardest things you can experience is to lose your narrative of yourself. We were highly incentivized as kids to present the "best" image of ourselves. That's how we stayed safe and in Mom and Dad's good graces. It felt like life and death to be seen by them as a good kid. Us traumatized kids often want to please everyone; we want to control how we are seen in specific ways. If we lose that carefully crafted narrative, we feel unsafe and that we've profoundly failed. I lost my own story on a national scale that day. Fox News was trying to accuse me of being a danger to children because I had a video that started with, "Hey, kids!" This kind of accusation has floated around LGBTQ people for decades, so it's not new. And I can remember being a kid and needing to fight that kind of stereotype. But I think a reporter from *Rolling Stone* wanted to interview me about this exact situation because accusations like that have become more intense over the past few years. Nowadays, people are accusing not just LGBTQ people of predatory behavior. If there was a way for me to learn that I shouldn't care what other people think about me, I can't imagine a more powerful lesson than being defamed like that on national TV.

Of course, Fox News's suggestions and insinuations about me are wrong. I know deep in my heart why I made these videos and what I was hoping to do. However, their segment was almost the opposite of the truth. During this incident, I felt like I was a kid again, seeing my parents accusing me of "making them late on purpose" or causing them harm or "doing something just to hurt them." The whole thing was a magnetic snap back to being six years old and not knowing why adults would accuse me of bad intentions. But this was on an enormous scale. Toxic parents will treat their children like adults with sinister motivations. And this Fox incident felt just like how my home felt growing up.

Toxic parents will treat their children like adults with sinister motivations.

By the way, I decided to make videos for kids for a very selfish reason. I wanted to heal my six-year-old self and my sixteen-year-old self. I wanted to reach young people with the message I never heard: *It's okay to be exactly how you are.* Making those videos was my way of reaching back through time to hold my hand and say, "Jeffrey, I love you. It's okay. All of who you are is beautiful." And so when people started accusing me—hundreds of thousands of people—of being dangerous, it was quite a shock.

The first video I did for kids was a huge success before the right wing and Fox News ever saw it. After I posted it, for the first two days or so the responses were all about parents sharing their experiences and posting videos showing them watching my video with their kids. I got parents putting my face next to theirs with their kids on their lap, everyone watching me as a family. It filled my heart with joy. It was a dream come true. What Jeff (if you haven't figured it out yet, yes, we're Jeff and Jeffrey) had said to me helped me remember that initial joy, and he helped me remember the point of the work that I do. My fulfillment is imperative. It is essential that I am happy with my work and myself. I must be full of myself in the best way possible! I must have joy and kindness in my life. I must be proud of how I'm changing the world. These things are much more important than trying to control the way others think of me.

A New Idea of Confidence

Confidence is such a weird idea. It's a tricky concept. Since hateful people come after me so often online (and sometimes on TV!), I get asked about confidence constantly, and the element of confidence that most people never bring up is that I was treated horribly as a child. I think what people want when they say they want confidence is to have gone through what I've gone through and come out the other side liking themselves. They want to be able to be maligned on Fox and then survive it. Of course, you *can* do that, though I wouldn't wish it on my worst enemy. If your life has gone down the route mine has, your parents or caregivers told you, at least on occasion, that you are horrible. Someone told you that you're worthless, whether with words or actions. And maybe even some other kids told you this growing up. Kids can be ruthless. But whenever I get asked about confidence, whenever I'm doing a book signing or I'm at a TV appearance, someone says, "How can I be confident like you?" And I immediately think about self-acceptance. Confidence seems to be shorthand in most people's minds for *persevering*, for acting decisively in all situations.

So, imagine this—you make a mistake at work. You do something with the best intentions, and it blows up in your face. You look incompetent, or close-minded, or like you intentionally gummed up. In that situation, most of us would go to work the next day and feel an incredible, crushing, deep, horrible sense of guilt, regardless of any external consequences. But imagine that you simply went to work the next day and *didn't* feel that way. What if you *didn't* self-punish for anything you've done or haven't done?

What if you were able to live the rest of your life without punishing yourself for all you've done "wrong"?

Part of the trickiness of the concept of confidence is that people want to feel a certain way—they want to feel like they don't have to worry about messing up. People think confidence is never having a self-doubting thought. Confidence is actually much closer to having a million self-doubting thoughts and moving ahead anyway. Going forward in your life without doubt is a false and impossible goal. But you can learn to stop the endless punishment and self-judgment for anything you do. Can you imagine a life where it's simply *okay* to have self-hating ideas without judging yourself for having them? Can you imagine a life where it's okay to have self-doubt? I want to emphasize this point, especially. Can you imagine a life where self-hate comes up strongly in your mind, and that's okay? Let's work through an example.

> **Confidence is actually much closer to having a million self-doubting thoughts and moving ahead anyway.**

You're at work, something goes wrong, and it's your fault. And your mind goes: "You're so stupid. They are going to laugh at you." Yes. This is how your brain can talk to you. It's ableist. It's awful. It's cruel. And until we look at it, we may not realize expressly how brutal it is. Imagine that happens to you. Your brain says you're stupid. And now, imagine you do nothing about that thought. Imagine you don't allow that thought or any of your reactions to bog you down. Imagine you don't get scared or paralyzed.

Also imagine that you don't believe you're the kind of person who deserves to hear pounding self-hate every day. What if the stuff that kept going on in your mind wasn't particularly interesting or relevant to you? That is, I think, what most people want. And that is, I think, what people mean when they say "confidence." They mean that they don't allow their negative thoughts about themselves to color their lives or their self-worth. So whenever someone asks me about being confident, and precisely when they ask, "How can I be confident like you?" I talk to them about the systems, the society, and the rules we grew up with that are beyond the individual. So we have self-hate in our heads. Your caregivers taught you to think certain things about yourself on a personal level. And there is also a society-wide, system-wide idea of who is *allowed* to be confident.

There is an overriding hierarchy of who can move on without self-punishment, of who is allowed to make a mistake and have that not mean a darn thing the next day. And it's only certain people who are allowed to experience that. If you're reading this, I guess you are not one of the people with this privilege. And I'm going to assume further that if you happen to be one of those people, you are sympathetic to people who are not those people. In other words, if you are reading my book, I'm going to assume you're not at the tip-top of the privilege pyramid. I'm going to assume that you are not the kind of person who was told and taught that they can ignore their mistakes, who was told and taught that they can forget how they treat other people. I'm going to assume that you do not get to try and fail a bajillion times, without it affecting your view of yourself as a person. Those people seem to exist, but I'm going to guess that's not us. I bring this up because saying "I'm not confident" is not a moral failing.

Let's Stop and Think for a Moment

What does confidence mean to you? If you were to draw a picture of a truly confident person, what would you include? What emotions or feelings go along with confident? Are there certain people who "get" to be confident and others who aren't allowed?

A popular parenting technique is to train children, at the youngest age possible, to parent themselves. Parents, caregivers, and authoritative people who were older than you needed you to enact a stern "inner parent," and not in a loving, kind way. Therefore, your lack of ability to let go of failures—to let go of mistakes—is not your personal deficiency. That idea, concept, and life was programmed into you from the earliest age. Authority figures required you to police yourself, to do a parent's job for them. And I'll make it ultra crystal clear right now: They wanted you to do the job of a bad parent for them. There is a possibility that a parent could instill confidence in their child by being kind to them, praising them, and helping them encounter failures and mistakes with an open heart. A parent could help their child fail with a sense of humor, with a sense that it doesn't mean anything about them or their character. That could happen, but it rarely does. What toxic parents want to train their children to do as quickly as possible is to police themselves, making the parents' duties more manageable. This (popular) parenting style is about dampening all of a child's complicated feelings or reactions, eliminating anything that might challenge a parent's authority. This kind of parenting is about extracting all the personality out of a child. These parents want their children to be under control.

Then, of course, there's confidence. And the concept of confidence plays directly into that style of raising children. Bad parents (often unwittingly) want their kids to be unconfident and, honestly, to constantly *try* to be confident. It's incredibly ironic, but I think you'll quickly find that if you give up trying to be confident, your inner sense of confidence will be stronger than before. Your concept of confidence (along with almost everyone else's) is about others. "I want to be confident," you say, and what you *mean* is, "I want other people to be impressed with me." You want to act so that other people will like you, respect you, and see you as valuable, worthy, better, and "confident." You want to, with a toss of the hair and a flick of the fingernail, be so big, bright, and colorful, to take no prisoners with your personality, for other people will see the value in who you are. To me, that's not absolute confidence. Any time your idea of confidence or your concept of self-worth (or your goal in life in any way, shape, or form) is tied to someone else, you are in deep trouble. As a child, you were set up to doubt your own worth and undermine any natural confidence you may have had.

So, let me give you an alternative definition of confidence: self-kindness, inner beauty, self-acceptance, soul grace, heart delight, self-care, and self-respect. I suspect this is what everyone truly craves. When a person asks me about confidence, they want the chance to love themselves unconditionally. They genuinely desire it. That is confidence. That is how to be confident: Be kind to yourself, no matter what happens, no matter how life goes.

If something happens at work, and it's a total failure, love yourself. That is the key to getting up and doing it again the next day. It's not about never having another self-doubting thought. The key to confidence is being kind to yourself no matter what happens. It is being able to love yourself enthusiastically and sticking with yourself in kindness from start to finish, from beginning to end, in every room and every situation, forever and beyond.

When I do TV, it's not that it's not nerve-racking, it's not that there's no energy coursing through my body, or that my heart rate doesn't go up. Having confidence doesn't mean you no longer experience nervousness. But because I'm confident in myself, in the deepest core of my being, no matter what anyone says, and most importantly (hello!) no matter what anyone else *thinks* about me, I know that I will have my own back. I know that I will like myself. I know that I will be kind to myself. I know that I will enthusiastically worship the core spirit of who I am.

Having confidence doesn't mean you no longer experience nervousness.

So, I'd recommend that you stop trying to be confident, especially if confidence means getting other people to be impressed. Stop trying to be confident, especially if confidence means meeting a certain standard before you can be happy. And certainly stop trying to be confident if confidence means you'll be the right, perfect person. It's much better to feel doubtful and have a safe place within yourself. It's better to experience, discuss, and clearly see your doubt, be okay with that doubt, fully embrace that doubt, and celebrate that doubt. If you can live with kindness in your heart, I'd rather have that than be 100 percent confident.

> **It's much better to feel doubtful and have a safe place within yourself.**

Let's Stop and Think for a Moment

What do you sacrifice in order to be confident? If being confident is one of your goals, what do you trade for being or seeming confident? Are certain behaviors or emotions off-limits when you think you need to seem confident? Can you be your whole self and still be confident?

The beautiful thing about not having an extremely comfortable life is that you have an excellent chance to become an entirely compassionate person. You see how your actions affect other people and how anyone's actions might affect the whole community. You care. Over the course of this book, I will be helping you learn how to take that compassion and care you have for others and apply it to yourself. Starting with confidence. The true definition of confidence is to care about yourself. Confidence is the act of folding yourself into how much you care. To me, being afraid of failure is a warped version of caring. It shows that you are concerned, care about how things go, care about what will happen next, and probably care about how your actions affect other human beings. But it is filled with fear. And the fear is misplaced. I would ask you to be most afraid of how your actions affect *you*.

It's a self-help cliché to "put yourself first." And I'm not necessarily recommending that. I'm asking you to put yourself *at least* on equal footing with everyone else. Care about everyone, and that includes yourself, right? But in those daily choice points, in those places where it's not clear, where you may not know what to do, always come back to caring for yourself. I think that's what people might mean when they say, "Put yourself first." Just make a self-caring, self-loving gesture if you don't know what to do. And within that, inside of that self-caring habit, is a kind of confidence that no one will be able to shake. If you can build an unwavering self-compassion, an enthusiastic love for yourself that becomes your default, that is the confidence you seek. And that will never leave you. And once that priority is clear, who cares if anyone else notices? At that point, who cares if anybody in the world knows how genuinely confident you are? So I'd rather have you stop trying to be fake confident. Stop trying to impress others. Stop trying to seem like you have it all together. Stop trying to meet a standard. Stop trying to get a favorable reaction. Stop all that stuff, especially if that's what "confidence" means to you.

Instead, turn around and include yourself in the care you already embody. Prove to yourself daily, moment by moment, breath by breath, situation by situation, that you choose to stay with yourself. Prove that you can stay with yourself in the most challenging circumstances. That is the ultimate power. That is the undermining of privilege structures in our culture. And that is confidence. Confidence means saying "I am with you" to yourself even when a national TV show devoted to hatred mocks you.

Go Ahead, Be Full of Yourself

The real reason that confidence is a false god is because confidence is irrelevant. Most of the time, people haven't stopped to consider what confidence really means or what it will even feel like when you get it. I can't speak for other people, but I often get *accused* of being confident. I assume people mean that I'm confident in a classic sense; they mean that I don't care what other people think of me. But what people see in me has nothing to do with what others think and everything to do with how I treat myself. I love myself unconditionally and people see that as confident. Of course, I'm me! I can't compare my experience to a "non-confident" Jeffrey! I only know that I want my whole life to be devoted to being kind to myself. I might seem like a walking billboard for a general idea of "confidence" because people can see right away that I've been through a lot of horrible stuff, and I've survived. It's sad to say, but many people like me don't make it, whether we are confident or not.

When I say "A lot of us don't make it," I mainly mean two things, one of which might surprise you. First, I mean we don't survive. We don't make it far into being an adult. People write to me constantly to say, "You remind me of my uncle, who's not around anymore." "You remind me of my cousin, whose parents found out that she wrote a love letter to one of her girl classmates, and she's no longer with us." Many people like me don't make it to see their forty-fourth birthday, as I have. But the other way people don't make it is by hiding. They don't show their true selves. They choose a life of what they think is safety, so that they can live. But what that "safety" ultimately means is that they do not get the feeling of freedom and joy that comes with being oneself. Even when being one's true self is frowned upon, even when who you are is looked down upon by your society. So when people look at me and they see confidence, part of that recipe for them is they assume (and in this case, it's a correct assumption!) that I had a rough time as a kid and that I've made a commitment to being myself anyway.

Despite everything, I chose to be my entire self. And despite how the world treats me today, I choose to be myself. For a marginalized person, being able to tell the truth of who you are is an outward display of what people usually assume is confidence. It automatically suggests a kind of bravado or self-esteem that many people don't have. What became most important to me was not "being brave" but being able to survive. I had to choose. Would I tell the truth, or not live to tell anyone everything? That experience taught me that if I'm going to stick around, I might as well enjoy it. I might as well be bold. I might as well be myself, and I might as well do everything I can to surround myself with people who know and respect who I am. They know what they're getting.

I feel it's necessary to say that I'm utterly grateful today, but I'm not grateful for what my childhood taught me. To be frank, I almost didn't make it. I'm not grateful that growing up as a nonbinary kid was so torturous that I felt like I had very few options. I would never say that's a good thing, even if the good in my life grew out of a lot of bad. What I *am* saying is that one good thing about my life today is the strength that came from that situation.

The underlying point is this: It is wrong to confuse that strength with something as surface level and mundane as most people's idea of being confident. In other words, I think it would be a mistake to conflate the absolute desperation of surviving against all odds with an egotistical sense that I could do no wrong or that everything I say is the right thing to say. I don't believe those things. I don't feel those things. It's, uh . . . quite the opposite. I know that there are many things I need to learn. I enjoy learning them. I know that everything I say is not perfect. And with that knowledge comes a doubling down on my commitment to being kind to myself. With that comes a doubling down on my duty to give myself a kind life.

I've learned to give myself the space *not* to feel confident. I touched a little bit on this irony before, but it seems that the word *confident*—what people may be reaching for when they use the word—means zero effs to give. People assume confidence comes from a total lack of reaction to other people's judgments of us. But confidence can be redefined. It can mean so much more. Your personal definition of confidence can be an ultimate self-acceptance. And that self-acceptance includes days and times and moments where you do not feel confident. If it's okay not to be confident, it's okay to learn. It's okay to fail and make mistakes. I define confidence this way and I know I will love myself regardless of any circumstance. You can know this too. You can see that you will love yourself tomorrow, no matter what happens today. And that is a gift I wish you would give yourself: the gift of setting aside the goal of "not caring what other people think of me" forever. Put aside the goal of trying to be everyone else's definition of confident. Give yourself the space to learn something, have something go unexpectedly, and have a different conversation within yourself. Can you achieve kind self-talk? Can you change the narrative you have about yourself inside your brain? Self-talk can be a horrible, hateful creature or a delightful angel. Stop asking, "How can I be confident? How can I do this right? How can I have the skill set?" Your self-talk is making things impossible for you. Your mindset isn't pushing for a rich, rewarding, or loving life.

The Monster Known as Self-Talk

It's time to change the way you talk to yourself. You must change how you talk *about* yourself and your life inside your head. It's very difficult to write a book like this, because I worry that your brain will use every sentence, word, and story to make your life worse. Even if I choose my words very carefully, I assume that—at least part of the time—your mind will use my words for the joy-thief called *comparison* (because comparison always steals our joy). I assume my words may be twisted and added to the list of what's wrong with you. Self-judgment is a habit (if you're like most people) that's nearly unavoidable. I assume that your brain will suck up my words into the ever-present, always-oppressive self-hate cloud that constantly rains on your shoulders.

Allowing self-hate to filter my world is something I have done for years. Every single bit of information that came at me that might have brought freedom, change, or relief into my life became a standard I used to beat myself up internally. This is classically known as *self-sabotaging*. But perhaps, even now as you read these words, the term *self-sabotage* brings up images of blame. You might even believe that your problems are your own fault and that everything would be great if you could just stop sabotaging yourself. Don't let a recognition of what trips you up become more fodder for self-hate. Don't let insight become a new standard for self-hate. Don't let any possibility for spiritual growth transmogrify into "Why can't you do that?" and "Why haven't you done that already?" I bring this up now to head it off at the pass. I want you to be aware. You can disregard any self-hate that might arise with what I'm about to say. Life isn't a contest or a reflection on you. And I'm not saying that changing your self-talk is easy. I'm not saying you should be "strong enough" or "good enough" or the best at changing your self-talk. I just feel compelled to let you know that it's *necessary*. Our lives are a series of stories we tell ourselves inside our heads.

Life isn't a contest or a reflection on you.

The quality of your life comes down to the narrative you have about yourself inside your mind. You might even say that your ability to focus correlates with your quality of life. Most people's attention is constantly on a cruel, horrible story about themselves. So, when I coach people one on one, when we talk over Zoom, when we have a frank discussion about what's going on in their minds, people get quiet. I need to use every ounce of charm and fun and jokes and batting my eyelashes to get people even to say—to repeat—some of the things that their brain tells them inside their head. I have a theory as to why this happens. It's probably because the inner dialogue, the internal talk, is so cruel that saying it out loud to someone else makes it abundantly clear how wrong it is. It becomes revealing. Once we say something like this aloud, its truly cruel, awful, and evil nature becomes evident.

Let's Stop and Think for a Moment

Take a day or two to record some of your self-talk. Carry your journal with you or use a note-taking app on your phone and write out some of the things you hear within your own mind. At the end of this time, look back over your list and ask yourself if that voice in your head is kind or not. How would you react if another, "outside" person said some of these things to you?

For example, if you're in a bad mood one day, and you snap at your partner, your mind may start making up wild scenarios. You know you didn't mean to lose control in the moment, but your head can multiply your guilt and you might even imagine your partner leaving you, or you dying alone. You might even imagine that you deserve loneliness.

Your mind may tell you that you're a horrible person, irredeemable, and that you can never change. Or that you're *selfish*. So, something as human and common as being in a bad mood is turned into a cruel inner monologue like this: *Your partner's going to leave you because you're weak and can't control your emotions, and you deserve to have your partner leave. You're unlovable.* And scene. It's cruel. It's internal violence. And we're supposed to hide it. We're supposed to keep it all inside.

If you had someone *outside* your head saying things half as cruel as anything going on *inside* your head, you would ditch that person. You would cut that person from your life as soon as possible. You would stop being in a relationship with that person. But this is coming from inside our head. Therefore, it is twice as cruel and believable. So you must change how you speak to yourself. You must change the inner dialogue.

When the hate is coming from inside our head, it is twice as cruel and believable.

When I was going on Newsmax TV, when the cameras were rolling and the interview began, I was saying inside my head: *I love you, Jeffrey. Thank you for doing this. I know this is not easy. I'm so glad you are here.*

Before leaving my apartment, while I was preparing to go to the Newsmax studio in Manhattan, I was kind to myself. I was getting ready, getting dressed, and saying, *Thank you, Jeffrey. You're beautiful. I'm so grateful for you.* And here's maybe the hardest thing I did that day. I said kind things to myself on the subway after that TV appearance. After I went through that challenging experience, being mocked and treated rudely on national TV, I remember riding home in self-kindness. It was the 6 train and my body was jazzy. I was shaking with lots of energy over what had happened. My heart rate was way up, *and* I repeated kindness inside my head, gripping the railing on that shaking, jerking train, saying, *Jeffrey, what you did today was brave. I am so grateful. You spoke up. I'm so grateful. You spoke out.* I was speaking to myself like a friend: "I admire you. I love you. Thank you for who you are."

This is very different from working with an affirmation or with a mantra. Affirmations can be aspirational: "People respect me. I am loved." But on the subway, I was not saying anything I *wished* was true or that might be true *someday.* And sometimes mantras are global. People repeat things like "May all beings be free" inside their heads. But I was being personal. That's what works for me and heals me. I've always found that saying things like "I'm glad you're here" to myself brings a vast comfort. Being directly and specifically kind to myself hits the immediate, desperate, beautifully sore spot my childhood gifted me.

Like telling myself "I love you." That heals wounds! For years, many people told me I was worthless. So nothing helps to soothe me like an inside voice saying, "I value you." Like any habit, changing the way I spoke to myself took a long time. Changing your self-talk will likely take time for you too. The old ways, the current ways you speak to yourself, will try to stick around. Your current self-talk may seem almost impossible to overcome, but it's worth trying to overcome it. It's worth the challenge. It's worth changing. It's worth taking every step imaginable—trying everything you can—to create a new habit of speaking to yourself with love.

You could try setting a timer. Then, when it goes off, you say something kind. You could hang up a sign with your favorite kind phrases on it. You could ask your friends to remind you. Use anything that works; it is worth trying. Heck, anything that *doesn't* work is worth trying because you will learn more about what does. Anything goes on your way toward a new sense of how to speak to yourself. And sure, you'll have challenging times when you'll fall into the old habit. You'll have days where you think poorly of yourself and feel the familiar blanket of your childhood self-hate habit. On those days, you'll hear inside your mind that you did the worst thing, that you're a horrible person. But those days will be fewer and fewer. I promise.

A word of warning: The evil and cruel way that society trained you—how you learned to treat yourself—is habitual. The system will not give up its power without a fight. But you are strong enough to make the change. And I hope that this book, this chapter, this moment, this sentence, and these words are your inspiration to make the change. I know that you can experiment with different kindnesses to tell yourself; you can make self-kind talk into a new habit. And I know that you can fight the evil pull into the old routine. That pull is simply how those around you trained your brain when you were growing up.

It's worth doing. The quality of your life, the sort of kindness you will live within, and the delightful self-respect will be worth any fight. And yes, the type of true, ultimate confidence you are craving will become your default, because it won't be about standards—yours or anyone else's. You'll be too busy living in love. That's what you deserve.

KEY TAKEAWAYS

1. It's okay to lose the narrative of yourself. Be careful that the stories you tell yourself about yourself aren't rehashes or lies you've been told about who you are.

2. Ditch the systems of self-punishment and guilt instilled in you in your childhood. Guilt is 100 percent useless.

3. Confidence is shorthand for the opportunity to love yourself unconditionally. If you hold yourself to an ever-changing standard, you will never achieve anything like confidence.

4. Self-cruelty is a habit. Habits can be broken.

Chapter 2

Stop Trying to Be Authentic and Start Speaking from the Authority of Your Experience

As I was writing this book, I realized that I was carrying around the idea that books aren't direct. They aren't up-front. I had a horrid case of writer's block bursting forth from a lifelong mythomania of what books should be. They needed to be "smart" and "poetic" and "grand." But I wanted to tell the truth plainly. So I decided to flip the script, my internal script. I simply wanted to share things I've encountered. I wanted to be plain and up-front. And I literally (and literature-ly) thought I needed to be "fancy" and grandiloquent from the start, or it wouldn't be an "actual book."

So, once I realized I was thinking that way, I recorded the chapters—just a voice memo on my phone. I decided I would act as if I were sitting down to have a conversation with a friend and talking about things that I find exciting, fun, and vital. And that gave the book the qualities I wanted it to have—it's conversational, entertaining, and accessible. I don't think those are good or bad things, but they are authentic to me.

What's *Your* Experience of Authenticity?

The idea of authenticity is *cloudy* for a lot of people. It's nebulous and keeps morphing and changing. For me, authenticity has always been wrapped up in LGBTQ phobia. Many of you know that LGBTQ-phobes often accuse trans people of being fake. I have been accused of being fake my whole life, ever since I was a little tiny kid and I started exhibiting the most fun (and femme) aspects of myself. So I began to be associated with inauthenticity, lying, and deception in other people's minds.

The assumption is people like me are pretending. We're the opposite of authentic because we're somehow hiding our true identity or hiding who we "really" are. As if we're pretending to be nonbinary—pretending to be LGBTQ. That's a pretty common accusation against people like me. And it took me a long time to see the association between this and larger issues like misogyny.

Within my career as a life coach, I see that many parents teach young women that their only hope—their only worth—is in serving others or at least deceiving others into thinking they have value. Does that make sense? Many women who I coach, talk to, and work with in workshops tell me about the beliefs their parents passed down to them, one being the only purpose women have in life is to get a man. The generation that raised them told them that a woman's place, and a woman's purpose, is to "get" a man.

And it wasn't until I started to dig into this with clients that I realized it goes a step deeper than that. Society teaches many women (like it teaches nonbinary people) that they are valueless and worthless. So the only way to get a man to value them is to deceive him into thinking there is some transactional value. She comforts him and serves him. She *offers* something. In other words, many of the women I've met and worked with go around with this deep, unseen, almost unconscious programming that their worth comes from men who find them valuable. And it goes further. They were told a simple message by society: "Be different, don't be the real you, and men will like you."

But also, many women learn that their only way to be *useful* to a man (as if they are ultimately worthless) is to trick him into it. Trick a man with inauthenticity. Trick him into liking you. This manifests, as you may know, as a mom teaching a daughter all kinds of tricks and tips and ways to talk and stand and present, to try to be something that they're not, so that a boy will like them: "Don't be authentic! You must learn to fake it." It's similar for people like me. The broader culture told me to do that with everyone—male, female, anyone. "Hide your authentic LGBTQ-ness, Jeffrey!" In my school and my church, everyone taught me to hide my authenticity so that people would see me as a valuable cisgender, straight member of society. That way, I would be "beneficial." To be beneficial, I must be inauthentic. I must pretend in order to please.

Let's Stop and Think for a Moment

Do you have any authenticity heroes? Do they always act perfectly or consistently? What qualities do you have in common with your heroes? Can you begin to see yourself as an authenticity hero, even with all your "flaws"?

The people I grew up around taught me many ways of *talking* small and *being* small. They taught me ways of hiding myself, to be more masculine, like a cis, straight man (three words that don't describe me!). In my first book, *How to Be You*, I told the story about my dad trying to teach me how to walk so that other kids wouldn't make fun of me. But what I never shared in that story is that, deep down in my heart, what I was really thinking was, *Please, Dad, tell me that you love me unconditionally. And tell me what you're doing to*

make society a safer and kinder place for kids like me.
And that's the part that a lot of parents don't get.

When I was in high school in the late eighties and early nineties, I dreamed of having a father who would tell me, "Don't worry. I'm going to talk to the other parents about kids who are bullying you. I will stand up for you because I love you exactly how you are." That's what I needed to hear! But his solution was a common one for parents at the time. His idea was "I'm going to teach you how not to be you so that you don't receive bullying." That "solution" made me feel crushed. What he was saying was that the problem was *me*.

The problem was always something I was doing, something I was, something deep-down wrong, bad, and ugly about me. And, of course, it wasn't a massive leap for me to get to "Ah, it's my me-ness. It's my queerness. I cannot hide my me-ness." Did you experience that too?

I'm not blaming my dad. And I don't have any ill will toward him. But the message was: *It's you.* Hide who you are, and people will like you. Hide who you are, and people will stop abusing you. Hide who you are, and people will stop being violent to you. It seems to me that many women and LGBTQ folks have that same message taught to them.

Immature or toxic parents will often treat their kids as *adults with bad intentions*. Parents who are self-absorbed or just don't have the skills for parenting (or the desire for parenthood) send this message: "It's you. Your intentions are bad. You're doing this on purpose."

So picture it: You're young and you're learning to tie your shoes. And you're having a hard time tying your shoes at the exact moment your parents want to leave to get to church. And you are, with fumbling fingers and tangled laces, holding the family up because you can't tie your shoes. That's when it happens. Instead of coming down to your level, sitting on the carpet, helping you tie your shoes, and saying, "I love you. Let's do this together," one of your parents says: "You're making us late on purpose."

Or they say something even worse: "You're doing this to hurt me." As a kid, we're unlikely to think, *Ummmmm, what? I'm doing what, exactly?* Instead, we just internalize the whole thing. We absorb the false accusation as true, and we feel awful. Now we know there is something wrong with us.

There's the planted seed, the origin of the concept that at five, four, or three years old, you are an adult with bad intentions. You're supposed to know everything and not be someone trying to hurt their parents instead of what you are: a kid who doesn't know what's going on and can't get their shoe tied.

So how does this all come back to authenticity? Being authentic is very tricky. We eventually learn that our way to be loved is by being ourselves. Unfortunately, our parents usually provide mixed messaging. We're getting this barrage of "Change yourself. Be something you're not. Hide who you are. Deceive people, and they will like you." But that is mixed with a cultural kind of doublespeak, the oversimplified greeting-card language of "Be you. Be authentic."

I've brought up LGBTQ-phobia and misogyny because people who do not suffer under humanity-wide systems of discrimination (i.e., straight, white, cis men) don't have a problem trying to be authentic. There is no cultural incentive to not be a man, for example. Without facing discrimination and phobia for your whole life, you may not even think about "being yourself." You are the walking default. Everyone else's "authenticity" is compared to you.

Let's Stop and Think for a Moment

Are you less than society's "ideal" in some way? Has this affected your ability to be yourself? Have you ever felt the need to perform or seem different than you naturally are because of society's judgments about you? What would happen if you stopped giving so much personal attention to the fake hierarchies of our current culture?

That's the point. To be someone like me—like us—and to be authentic is risky behavior. I tried for years to be perfect instead of authentic. I tried to be the ideal Christian, kid, and student. I mistakenly thought perfection would be a shield. If I were perfection, I wouldn't get disciplined (or worse). The whole time, I knew I was lying. I wasn't perfect, and I could never admit it. Remember, I was the one who learned every single Bible verse I possibly could. If people were talking about judging others, I could exclaim, "Matthew 7:1 says . . ." and on and on. I rehearsed these conversations in my head for hours on end!

And again, I knew it was all a lie. I knew I didn't like the Bible. I knew I was LGBTQ from a very early age. As a six-year-old, I knew that God (deep breath) was disgusted by me because of who I am. So of course I was pretending not to be me. And I was angling, for example, to be a perfect little Bible scholar so that I would not get hit. My ratiocination was precise. My logic was sound. I wanted to be perfect so my mother would not reject me and so my father would not judge me. I did not want to be shamed by them. All significant incentives to pretend! And if you're like me, when you hear the message that you're supposed to "be yourself" to be happy, it really packs a punch. Some people on this earth never go through what I just described. They never experience spending so much brain power every day fighting to compensate for what's "wrong" with them.

But ironically, if someone doesn't go through what I've gone through, they never get to blossom into choosing authenticity against all odds. So, what I went through isn't fair, but I'm happy to be me because I now have an unshakable sense of who I am. I have what I call *earned authenticity*. And I assume that if you're reading this book, you have earned authenticity as well, or you're ready to choose it.

Depending on how you grew up, you might have learned that being yourself and telling your truth was synonymous with real physical danger. In anyone's mind, and especially a kid's mind, it's not that big of a leap to say, "If I tell the truth, my parents will reject me. If I tell the truth, I'll be out on the street and dead."

I guess it's weird to write it out like that, to lay it all out so clearly, but it does get that deep. "If I tell my whole truth, I'm in danger." It got that deep for me when I was a kid.

But once we get over that childhood fear of being authentic and truthful, one of our subsequent pitfalls is *trying* to be authentic. You may have grown up with zero examples of how to be authentic. You may be so used to pretending to be someone you're not just to be liked that you don't know what authenticity is. You never explored authenticity, you may not know much about it, but you still set it up as a goal. It's okay to set it aside for a time. You may be much better off with a different focus for now. And that's why I speak about authority. Authority, in my mind, is something you give yourself. Authority is something you already naturally have. There may be other people who listen to you. There may be other people who respect you. There may be other people who find value in your message. But whether you have the *authority* to tell your truth is a gift you give yourself.

> **Whether you have the *authority* to tell your truth is a gift you give yourself.**

One of the self-help phrases I just cannot stand is "Fake it till you make it." I think what people are trying to say with that phrase—what they want you to do—is trick your brain into a new reality. You've been told a lie about yourself. And so the theory of this advice goes, what you want to do is act out the truth until your brain can catch up. But faking it is what you were taught to do in the first place to get validation from others. So instead of performing your truth until it becomes your truth, I think you should do the real spiritual heavy lifting of listening to yourself, embracing yourself, and then putting your authenticity into action.

Say what you are here to say. Say what is necessary for each situation. Be open about who you are. Be honest about your reactions and needs and feelings. Be willing to roll with yourself, with others, and with situations. Be ready to be open.

There's a piece to this that I'm hesitant to write. I'll get to this more in-depth in a later chapter. But one thing about authenticity that scares almost everyone is that authenticity is about having *needs*. When you are fully authentic, you are also open about what you need, who you need it from, and when. And we were all taught that having needs is a dangerous and vulnerable position to be in. And many of us are used to self-delusion: having needs in private but trying to present a "brave" front. We never learned to be congruent in our psyche. We never learned that type of freedom.

Dad's Tires, Again

I remember learning to be free. I was self-taught. I would twirl around and have the most fun whenever nobody was home. I can't tell if it was a good thing or a bad thing, but I was left alone for stretches of time when I was a young kid. My siblings are much older than I am. My brother and sister were born very close together, and then I was born about six years later. I sometimes speculate that it was not a planned pregnancy because of that gap. But I also assume it because of the way my parents treated me when I was a kid. I can't decide if being alone was a good or bad thing, because when I was left alone, I got to be myself. I got to be this beautiful, authentic, shining rainbow child who would wear my sister's clothes or things that I had gotten at thrift stores or that I'd . . . acquired . . . from the community theater when I would do plays. And I would be all alone, and I would twirl around and feel so happy and so delighted.

I became a double agent.

I was a happy, free, twirling, beautiful child. I also became the perfect quick-change artist. If you're unfamiliar with the theater, quick changes happen when a character exits one scene and then very quickly enters the stage again in a different costume. The actor will walk offstage, and Velcro will rip as the first costume comes off and another one comes on. When I was a kid, what I was always quick-changing was myself, inside and out. I would go from alone-time Jeffrey in beautiful, glittering, gorgeous twirl-twirl dresses into the "perfect son" costume. I went from a gown to a T-shirt and jeans, pretending to do my homework in under thirty seconds. I was resourceful. As I mentioned, I distinctly remember what my parents' tires sounded like because that sound was so important for my safety. I was a double agent because I would dress up glittery, having fun all by myself, until I heard that crunch on the gravel. Then the magic. I would rip at my clothes and run for the living room, ready to play the part of "perfect little boy." I would rush onto the couch and open a textbook just as Dad opened the front door.

I was also a double agent because I devoted my brain space to two different things. I could have the authentic, playful moments while being constantly on alert for those tires on gravel. I had learned that there was an innate playfulness within me. I had worked out how to express myself, play, and be free, and how to have these moments of glory that certainly helped me survive my childhood. Half of my brain was devoted to the freedom I felt when the pressure was off—having fun and being glamorous. And the other half of my brain was dedicated to the quick change—to keeping myself safe through deception So, part of my identity was about expressing myself authentically. And the other part was about framing and excusing and pretending to deflect from who I authentically am. I carried both of these parts around with me for years. They fought each other.

When I went to the monastery, I learned to give the inner mitigator, my inner judge, a new job, not based on fear but on talent. I learned to let that part of who I am off the hook for hiding my authenticity. There was intelligence in that split mind from my childhood. I had to have my wits about me to survive. There was a craftiness there. Young Jeffrey designed a real quick change. And so I made a deal with that part of me. I said, "Let's use your wits."

I told myself that I would use that craftiness to help other people, and use that cunning and intelligence to help make art. I didn't need to be afraid or "think fast" to survive anymore. I decided to use my talents for storytelling and more, to break hearts, connect with people, and write books instead of using it to hide the twirling, dancing, loving, singing, theatrical, beautiful Jeffrey. I decided to use that intelligence to open up about who I am, to elevate myself, to help tell the stories that needed telling. I used the intelligence I learned through trauma to unearth what I wanted to show the world and what needed to be shared. In other words, I used what I learned through my trauma to help me become a more pure, more authentic *me*. And I truly needed those young life talents to tell my story authentically. One thing I learned through years of trying to convince people that I'm not how I am, is what the truth really is. I earned an ability to help, connect, and tell the human story for maximum togetherness. I learned how to make space for other people in empathy. I learned how to help people see others' struggles as their own. And those talents have served me well ever since.

If you have a part of you that is still helping you hide, I don't blame you. And I can't blame your parents or society. I don't think any part of you is terrible, but it might be that the parts you're using to hide are better suited to another purpose. Today, it might be time to put some of that intelligence toward helping you live within the freedom of an authentic life. I transitioned out of being divided, living within the prison of an emotional binary. I transitioned from dressing up and hiding alone to dressing up in public. Now I do it on the internet! I do it on national TV! And I needed that mitigator and inner storyteller to help the authentic, beautiful, vulnerable, and soft parts of me be safe. I'm not saying that transition was easy, but it's the most critical work I've ever done in my life.

The parts you're using to hide are better suited to another purpose.

And part of that came from dancing in the barn, twirling and drinking in my freedom. I had no clue that I was strengthening something important within me, that all the while I was laying the foundation for a lifetime of giving myself permission to play and sing for hay bales. I became a quick-change artist of the mind with no one around, getting down to my play and free-form expression with speed and grace. I became an authority on how to be myself safely. And I never realized I had that power over myself until years later.

Enjoy the Authority You Have

When people think about authenticity, they sometimes think of a light, fun version of the word. Authenticity is freedom. There's an implication that being your authentic self is easy breezy. Why wouldn't you just choose to be all of who you are? Instagram makes it seem effortless. This always irks me a bit. The concept of authenticity is so textured, so layered, and it can be a heavy and deep subject for the many of us who have fought to be ourselves. So, let's establish how complex and challenging it might be to "be yourself."

A personal history of being judged and disciplined teaches many of us that who we are (on an intense level) is wrong and bad and should be hidden. That's number one. Number two: When people use the word *authenticity*, they usually mean a certain comfort level. They mean you could sit in front of a group of people and just be yourself without too much trouble, with a lot of ease. And so, if people don't have that ease, they're thought to be "inauthentic," or worse. Maybe they feel that their anxiety means they could never and should never be their whole selves. If people don't have ease, they assume that they can't be authentic, or that they might feel the need to act deceptively if anxiety makes them want to hide. Some folks might even think that, without an ability to achieve "authenticity," there might be something shameful or wrong with them. If someone can't have that kind of natural, flowing, "be yourself" energy, they might be deficient somehow.

Let's Stop and Think for a Moment

Try an experiment. For one day, assume you belong in every room you enter. For every work meeting and social event for that day, digital or in-person, assume that you are meant to be there and that you are a valued contributor to the situation. What would change for you if you regularly assumed that the natural you was wanted everywhere?

Number three: The definition of authenticity can be different for different people. Its meaning can be slippery and changeable. So, no matter how authentic you are, no matter how much you're being yourself, your mind might still accuse you of not being yourself "enough." For example, I get accused of being inauthentic on social media constantly. It's partly because I'm nonbinary, and people associate that with fakeness. It's partly because of people associating being trans with deception. But it's also that people often dislike what I have to say, or they disagree with me. But of course, opposing what someone has to say is not the same as that person being inauthentic.

So, when I think of authenticity, and all these layers, I want you to understand why and how the concept might be tricky and complicated for you. I want you to consider why and how "being authentic" might be elusive for you. And it might be a changing and changeable concept for you. Being authentic is hard. At least one of the reasons that being authentic is tricky is because we're afraid that our friends will reject the actual, authentic us. A few moments ago, I said that there is nothing wrong with you. I stand by that. But you're right. You probably will be rejected. Surprise! No matter what we do, how we act, or what we say, people will have an issue. I tried for so long to be the perfect person, to make the ideal videos on the internet that nobody could fault. I wanted to make videos that nobody would find lacking. I wanted people to find nothing negative to say. On the internet! I tried to be perfect and please hundreds of thousands of followers at once. I took people-pleasing to the most prominent, galactic level.

And let me tell you what I learned. It's impossible. If you're going to be truly authentic, you're going to speak your mind. You're going to say a truth that you have observed. People are going to dislike you. Not always, but a lot of the time! I find the concept of authority to be much more critical. It's a much more engaging and clarifying focus. Because if I say, for example, nonbinary people are not treated well in modern American culture, and someone argues with that statement, it means very little to me. If I think of what I said as speaking from the authority of my experience, then somebody has a problem with *my experience*. It feels like they have

a bias against nonbinary people. And that's something I don't need to take personally. It's a much different ball game. It's a much different interaction with "hat-
ers" if what they seem to
have a problem with is
the authority of my expe-
rience. Because that just

Authenticity is worth it, even if others try to make it an unpleasant choice.

means they have a different experience. They don't respect my authority, and that's plain old bias, which, believe it or not, is fine with me. I know there are many people who don't respect my experience, and I understand why they don't. They are bigoted, or their upbringing has taught them fear. That doesn't bother me. But when it becomes personal, when it becomes individual, when it becomes about hating me expressing my authentic, beautiful Jeffrey heart and someone stomping all over it, that is a highly unpleasant experience. And that unpleasantness goes hand in hand with how I experience authenticity. Authenticity is worth it, even if others try to make it an unpleasant choice.

But when I permit myself to speak freely about the *authority* of my experience, that is a self-kind, self-respectful, self-powerful place to speak from. When I talk from the power of my knowledge, people may get confused. I may learn to use better or more *inclusive* language or different, clearer language. As long as I am speaking from that place of authority, there is no room for others' judgment about my personhood and my authentic nature. If I communicate clearly from my own experience, there is little room for a conclusion about what is or is not "authentic Jeffrey." There is little room to review what I have to offer as a human and whether it's valuable. The reason that you have authority is that you have lived. You have years of experience with your perspective on life. You have a point of view in which you are an authority, and that's the key to answering these questions: What is it like to have your life? What has it been like to be you so far? And, of course, your experiences incentivized you to deny that you had any experience whatsoever. Depending on your parents, it was all about *their* experience. It was all about *their* truth. They wanted you to believe that they were imparting wisdom to you. There was never any room for dialogue or difference or your own experience.

And it's time to learn a new lesson. You've got to *enjoy* the authority you have and recognize the value of your voice. You must internalize that you know truths that can benefit other people. If you're too busy *trying* to *seem* authentic or even trying to be a version of authentic, you are not sharing the absolute truth of what it is like to be you as a human being. You're not helping someone else broaden their understanding of what it means to be a human being. And that's a true gift that gets lost in the cheap Instagram discussion about being authentic.

Enjoy your authority. Have joy. You see, you can be authentic for the heck of it, for fun, or because you feel like it or want to. Your authenticity can bring you a lightness, a glow that allows you to shed burdens you may not even know you had. This shift is serious work in the sense that it's essential, but that doesn't mean you need to continually approach it with a heavy heart and a "good reason."

On Having "Good Reasons"

You must know by now that you have good reasons for everything. At least, you have reasons that make sense to you, within you, for everything you do. You constantly walk around with explanations for what you do. You may not know what they are in each moment, but they are there. And I'll tell you about a spiritual principle that changed my life and made it so much easier for me to grow, change habits, and have the life I want: You don't have to have a *good* reason for anything in particular. If I could flip a switch for anyone, whether I teach them in a workshop or talk to them on the street, it would be to help them see that the reasons for their actions are *already* genuine, good, important, or at least just human. One common motivation for people to do anything is to meet an unmet need. What's the classic one? Oh, yes, dating someone unkind . . . Somebody dates someone abusive, or perhaps they've dated a string of mean folks who are awful to them. And they probably assume (if their parents programmed them, like most of us were) that this pattern is *their* fault. It's a character flaw. "If I could just learn not to do this, I'd be perfect. Why am I like this? It's because my father did this or that . . ." And on and on and on. Instead of assuming you have a standard human reason (trying to meet an unmet need), you might believe you have bad motives or bad intentions. You might believe you're weak or an awful, flawed person yourself.

But in this example about dating, maybe you're just constantly trying to meet the need we all have: to be loved and accepted. And so you're trying to date people who seem, at first, like they will love and accept you for who you are. And you think, "Great! I'll finally be loved!" But of course it goes south soon afterward. And the classic "self-improvement" thing to do is find the wrong logical reason you keep dating jerks. I always encourage everybody to choose a different approach. Find the good, reasonable, and human explanation— the *valid* reason you have for repeating any behavior. Or, at the very least, assume you have a valid reason, whether you can see it or not. You'll be better off that way.

I'll lay an even more profound truth on you, one that took me years to learn: You cannot see the real reason for something until you assume it's a valid reason. I know what I'm talking about, because for a while I was stuck in the pattern I just mentioned. I had an unkind father who was physically and emotionally abusive. And I dated a series of jerks. And I judged myself for it harshly. I thought I was unintelligent. I assumed that it was because I was just replaying a childhood pattern, and I better get over it. I assumed that I was weak or that I had some lousy reason. I must be too awful to get out of the pattern, or I had some other flaw.

It wasn't until years later that I realized I had a valid, good reason. Not to oversimplify me, but I was trying to heal my childhood wounds by reliving their pattern. I wanted to feel better. I wanted to be happy. The crux of the behavior was that I was trying to find a version of my dad and make that dad into a good, loving person. I was trying to find healing. That's a good thing to want! That's a good reason to date someone! And I happened to be looking in the exact opposite place where I would find healing. I could see all this once I accepted that my reason was good—that I was a good human trying my best. After that, I could see that it was okay and even lovely to want love and be motivated by love.

Let's Stop and Think for a Moment

What are some of the "good reasons" for existing that you carry with you? Is there any internal argument that you are still having with your parents even though they may not be a constant presence in your life? How would it feel to do most things—or anything—without a reason or excuse?

Of course, expecting a jerk to change is often a recipe for a long wait. Once I realized that I was trying to bring healing into my life via other people, I turned my attention toward the actual healing. I decided to read the books, talk to the therapists, go to the workshops, seek the activities that would heal that part of my life. And then, having noticed my good motivations and having focused on healthily meeting that need, I could be free to date nice people who weren't jerks. As part of that new goal, I made a list of ten things I wanted in an actual healthy partner. I had a good reason for dating these awful people, and I wanted to clarify how to work with the excellent reason without dealing with the horrible people. I realized I didn't want to use the people I was dating to relive my childhood stuff anymore—I didn't want to spend my whole life trying to get the healing I needed through other people, particularly the sort of people who are not wired to give it. And I wanted to try to heal my childhood effectively.

Trying to meet a need through someone who can never help you meet it is stunningly inefficient, and the heartbreak that comes from those failed relationships is devastating. I remember thinking, *Maybe I want to avoid all that.*

So, I decided to visualize the partner I wanted. That way, if they walked into the room, I would know it's them. And I wouldn't push them aside as I'm rushing to try and date the biggest jerk in the room. I made a list of ten things I wanted in a partner. I assumed I had excellent and pure reasons for wanting love, and I asked for the best the universe could bring to me. I still have the list. It had attributes like "somebody who's physically active," "somebody who's financially stable," "somebody who supports me as an artist, and gets my identity." It wasn't necessarily the most profound list, but it was what my heart wanted. I did want someone with a sense of humor and more. And then Jeff messaged me on OkCupid. My brain knew he wasn't a jerk, and therefore, my brain wanted to get rid of him immediately. Ah, but I had made a pact with myself to honor my good reasons for dating. I vowed that anybody who had eight of the ten attributes on my list (and Jeff had ten of the ten) I would go on three dates with and then reassess if this person would help me fuel my new obsession with healthy growth.

But my brain didn't even want to go on a date with Jeff. I remember looking at his profile, looking at our direct messages, all of it. And I was thinking, *Oh, a nice guy. Ew. No thanks.* But I had this rule and this pact with myself. I had this list, and I was like, well, I guess I'm going to try another date with this guy who has all ten attributes. We've been together for eleven and a half years. Last year, we were still so in love that we got married on Zoom during a pandemic.

After being together for so long, I can see that my list was a way for me to figure out what is authentically meaningful—to clarify exactly what was right *for me*. It was telling the truth to myself about who I really am and what I deserve. I ultimately had a "good reason" for dating jerks. I was trying to heal something, and it wasn't working. It was the wrong method. I didn't know any better, and that was okay. Love is ultimately always a good reason. It's a good rule of thumb to assume you have a reasonable motivation for anything you do. You can also assume your patterns and your spiritual growth pain points are there for a good purpose. And, in accepting that your base

It's a good rule of thumb to assume you have a reasonable motivation for anything you do.

motivations are authentically, wonderfully *good*, you can shine a light on the true reasons behind your patterns and redirect them to a healthy purpose. You are a good person with good motivations. And you can learn to heal yourself and hone your good reasons healthily.

KEY TAKEAWAYS

1. Your presence and value are not dictated by your "worth" or "use." Being "useful" is not a prerequisite for your respect or value as a human being.

2. Authentic is not the same as perfect. Your journey to authenticity can be messy and meandering.

3. Coming to terms with your version of authenticity is worth it, even if others judge

you or try to make honoring your version
of authenticity an unpleasant choice.

4. Reasons for our patterns are often less wrong
   than we think. Get out of thinking that reasons
   can be good or bad. Your unique reasons can
   be beautiful and fully human.

Chapter 3

Stop Saying "I Don't Know What to Do" and Start Admitting That You're Just Afraid to Do the Wrong Thing

High School Dance

In high school, I was popular only once. I wasn't popular for only one *year*, for one *month*, or even for one *day*, but just one time, for about thirty seconds. I was generally a sparkly kid, even though I knew that I needed to hide that sparkle to be safe at a young age. Or *try* to hide it. Sadly (and eventually happily), I was never very talented at hiding. School was rough. Many days, I faced violence at the school, and then I would go home and sometimes face violence there. Years later, in a glorious bid to "rosify" our past, Mom told me, "I always thought you were so brave. I never knew where you got the courage to be yourself." While I was trying to hide, I was obvious. If she had thought I was brave when I was a kid, she never said so. And she never treated me like a brave hero. But I was fearless in one unquestionable way: I stopped trying to hide early. I came out to Mom when I was eleven.

I flat-out told Mom who I was with the only language I could comprehend. I told her, "I think I like boys." Unfortunately, she was immediately angry. She didn't call me brave. Instead, she figuratively slammed my closet door shut, yelling about how I was too young to understand what I was talking about. Her face was red. "Don't ever say that again."

So I didn't. For years. Eventually, getting less and less talented at hiding as time passed, I tried a fumbly bumbly re-coming-out around age sixteen, with similar results. But by the time I was a senior in high school, I honestly couldn't stand hiding anymore. I wanted to take a metaphorical screwdriver to the hinges of my closet door. At eighteen years old, I wanted there to be no way I could go back in. I came out to everybody, whether Mom wanted me to or not. At church. At school. I told Grandma. (Grandma was *eccentric*, and she said, "I thought you were bi because you have both ears pierced.")

I know "all at once" is not everyone's trajectory or style when it comes to coming out, but it was the only way I could think of to assert myself and make my truth stick. I hated that decision. I was jealous of the straight kids I knew who didn't need to decide to come out. But I told the truth universally, and I said it loudly. Once I was out at school, once I had made that choice, I had another massive decision in front of me: Would I participate in my high school's senior year Sadie Hawkins dance?

What's a Sadie Hawkins dance, you say? It was an odd tradition at my school, based on a newspaper comic, where we had prom in the spring, but in the fall we had a weird, topsy-turvy, "the world is turned upside down" dance, where the girls asked the boys out. Evidently, boys were *supposed* to ask girls to a dance. That's what was *supposed* to happen. I didn't know this back then. And the whole gimmick of the fall dance was the lunacy of a girl asking a guy out. Girls asking guys! How weird! I also found out years later that Sadie herself, described in the comic strip as "the homeliest gal in them hills," desperately asked boys out on dates. And she was ostracized for that decision.

And so, because the asking out was reversed, *all* the traditions were turned around. Instead of a prom queen with her queen's court and her date, we had a fall dance *king* and his court and his date, the fall dance queen. The king and queen, no shocker, were the most popular kids in school. If you were a boy (or everyone thought you were, heyyy) at my school in Spring Grove, Pennsylvania, you could either be a farmer or a football player.

And the king of the fall dance was always the football captain . . . the most popular boy. Go figure.

The football captain won king of the Sadie Hawkins dance in a landslide. But to my surprise, I won the election too. I didn't find out until months later that the kids thought it would be hilarious to go around behind my back and vote for me. The court was a popularity contest, and I was deeply unpopular, and the mismatch was a great joke to my fellow students. So the kids in my high school—since I had come out, since I was so very, very LGBTQ—thought it would be a laugh riot to plot and plan, to turn their heads and whisper among each other, "You should vote for Jeffrey Marsh to be on the fall dance court. It'll be hilarious."

The day they announced who won spots on the fall dance court over the PA system in homeroom, they said my name. I questioned what it meant. Did I get . . . votes . . . really? I was shocked and stunned and a little weirded out, and a little suspicious. I couldn't decide whether I should participate in the court or not. I kept saying, "I don't know what to do."

I wanted the other kids to see that someone like me could boldly exist.

But then it occurred to me: I came out for a reason. I decided to be me for a reason, openly. I wanted to show what it was like to be someone like me. As unpopular as I was, I wanted the other kids to see that someone like me could boldly exist. That may be a naive approach to coming out, but it made sense to me. It was the nineties, after all. So, there weren't that many examples of what it was like to be LGBTQ, let alone gender nonconforming, especially not in my rural Pennsylvania high school.

All of that was why I had decided to come out in the first place. As my mom said, I guess I had gumption, but that decision hadn't been hard for me. I'd known what to do then. And I did it because I wanted to make the world better for me and anyone like me. That decision was still ringing in my mind now, playing over and over again as I thought about whether to accept my election to the fall court. When I told my parents, "I don't know what to do. I don't know what to do. I don't know what to do," about the fall dance court, I kept thinking, *Here's my chance to show them . . . me.* And so I decided to go for it. I looked to my heart and my heart said yes. I don't know how else to explain it, but my heart was telling me: "Go for it. Go ahead. It might be a risk. You might make the wrong decision, but that seems like the way to go in your heart." It turned out to be one of the most challenging times of my young life. *And* one of the most glorious.

We were standing together, the five members of the court, four boys with their four dates, and me. I was alone. Ahhh, I was always alone at that age. We were all standing in the hallway under an archway of a white lattice with fake flowers stapled onto it. The multipurpose room (it was an underfunded school, and this room was part cafeteria and part gym and part whatever else) was buzzing with student excitement. An assembly! The entire high school student body filled the multipurpose room. It was a big day. All kids like being out of class for special occasions. All kids except me, maybe. My palms were sweating, and my heart was beating through my chest.

They were getting ready to announce us as the fall dance court. At the front of our row was the king, the captain of the football team, and his date. In the spring, she would become prom queen. A teacher was holding a mic, faking being excited to announce the winners of the class election. The teacher said the name of the captain and his date, and the two of them walked out. Everyone started to applaud. It was the kind of strained enthusiastic applause reserved for trying to impress the most popular kids.

The king and his date walked to the center of the room, where they both turned to wait for the rest of us to enter. All the court members would line up with their dates. The students would applaud. And that would be the presentation. After that, we'd go off to whatever our next period was. They announced the second court member and his date. Everyone applauded and I thought I might puke.

There I was, standing in the archway alone, waiting for them to call my name. My breath was fast and caught in my throat. I still didn't know if going through with this was the right decision.

I didn't know what would happen next. When you're in high school, everything is dramatic and amplified. And

I was feeling everything at once. My emotions turned everything up all the way. I had no idea if what I was doing was good, bad, right, wrong, perfect, or imperfect.

The only thing I knew was that I was next and that I was nervous as heck. The teacher was about to say my name. The kids were silent. I had a fist in my throat, tightening around the tears. And then . . . I felt . . . a presence. Someone was right behind me, over my left shoulder. I knew that there were couples behind me, the remaining members of the court, but this felt different. There was an additional energy. I slowly turned to look, my body frozen, only my neck twisting around. I saw him. It was the captain of the football team. It was the popular kid—the king. He reached out and took my left hand. *What?* He put my left hand into the crook of his right elbow. *What is happening?* I heard the teacher inside the multipurpose room, ". . . and Jeffrey Marsh." And then we both stepped forward. The fall dance king escorted me out into the group of kids, my peers; he led me out into the room in front of the whole student body. The Bangles echoed from the school's crappy speakers: "Am I only dreaming? Or is this burning an eternal flame?" *Is this magic? Is this a dream?*

Everybody was laughing. The other kids pointed and howled. The room was the definition of a teenage nightmare. It turned into (maybe) the worst thing that can happen to a young person in high school. The football captain began to "act femme." He was saying "Ooooh, hello" in a high voice and fanning himself, bending his wrists into a gay stereotype. He was mocking me. This made the students laugh even harder.

That dream was so big that it eclipsed the nightmare.

But—and I know this sounds weird—I didn't find out about most of this until later. I didn't realize in the moment that I was being mocked and laughed at, because I was still back in the magic. The dream had caught me. It was the dream of being escorted by the most popular boy in school. I felt alive. I felt free. And I felt happy. I was queen for a day for the first time in my life, and nothing could hurt my glee. I know the whole situation sounds like a nightmare, but it was also a dream. A bittersweet nonbinary happy/sad fantasy. And, at least at first, that dream was so big that it eclipsed the nightmare. I have no idea what my face looked like, but I remember feeling seven feet tall and happy.

I wouldn't understand until later that I felt happy because of the affirmation of my gender, because of the affirmation of who I am. I was being my true self, and that affirmation filled the world as I knew it. The feeling of being escorted by the most popular kid in school, being witnessed, and being his "date" for a moment was one of the most profound and beautiful moments of my life. I didn't hear the kids laughing at me until a few moments later. I didn't get the "joke" that is me, until later. And that's partly why that moment is something I treasure today. It is so beautiful to me, even though it ended up being incredibly painful. But the beauty was in learning how being affirmed and seen can erase the need to "protect myself." An affirmation can obliterate an error. Did I make a mistake? Should I have not come out? Should I have stayed small and not participated in the court ritual? No. By deciding to follow what my heart said was right, and by putting myself out there as the real *me*, I learned a significant lesson: I deserve that affirmation. I give myself that affirmation today. I give myself that kindness. I treat myself, inside, as the most popular kid in school. And that makes any anxiety, any stress about making a right or wrong decision, seem puny.

I know that I can stay in a beautiful, gorgeous, and affirmed place without seeing or caring that other people are metaphorically (or actually) laughing at me. That day planted seeds. I have learned never to wonder if I've made a mistake or not. It's not worth it. Instead, I have learned how to stay affirmed with the beauty of feeling alive. I realized at a certain point that I must give myself that beautiful dream of 24/7 affirmation. I didn't need the kids. I didn't need my parents. I didn't need a boy paying attention to me. I didn't need anyone to give me permission to take ownership of who I am.

I didn't need anyone to give me permission to take ownership of who I am.

Staying with that affirmation, that self-adoration from start to end through any decision, helps me stay in a place of clarity. Today, I live in a position of assumed belonging. I stay in an area of celebration and light, no matter what choice I make. I stay there no matter how a decision plays out. And I stay there no matter what truths I tell.

You Know More Than You Think

The title of this chapter is so mean: Stop Saying "I Don't Know What to Do" and Start Admitting That You're Just Afraid to Do the Wrong Thing. I'm not supposed to talk that way. All the same, I find the words to be empirically valid. I stand behind the chapter title as a true statement and a good bit of advice. And I don't want it to get swallowed into self-hate. Spiritual practice and self-growth are not about forcing the scared, tiny, childlike parts of yourself to suck it up and do stuff anyway. So, that's not what I'm saying in this chapter. What I *am* saying is that there's a bigger truth to find in decision-making. Your fear of making a wrong decision is the *ultimate* bad decision. The fear of getting in trouble *is* your trouble. None of us have all the answers. It's okay not to know something, and it's okay if you feel uncomfortable when you have to make a decision. The way I look at it is sometimes deadlines are deadlines. Sometimes an answer is needed on a specific day at a particular time. But often, that's not the case. Many, many times, it's okay to wait for clarity. When Jeff and I first started dating, that was one of the things that he liked most about me. Whenever I couldn't decide something, I specifically used that phrase: "I'm going to wait for clarity."

And he started saying it as a semi-joke with his friends. "Where do you want to have dinner? Oh, let's wait for clarity." But eventually, that phrase became as natural to him as it was to me. He got used to, even addicted to, the luxury of waiting until a decision was clear enough that it *made itself*. The universe has a way of letting you know when a choice needs to be made and which choice to make. If we can learn to listen and grow quiet within and set aside the clanging dramatic voices in our heads, we go in the direction life wants us to. Of course, this means being able to wait if it is not yet time to decide.

Let's Stop and Think for a Moment

Consider waiting for clarity in your own life. Is there an unresolved upcoming decision that brings you stress? Is it possible to put that decision off until you have more information or until an answer becomes more obvious? Why does the decision have to be made now? What will happen if you wait?

When I studied at the Buddhist monastery, I quickly learned that we rarely actually make decisions. It seems like we are in charge and that we are "at fault" for how our life goes, but that is an illusion. Sometimes during decision-making, if I can't see the broader picture that life is calling me to, I feel like a little child: "It's all up to me." And yet, there is always energy to life. Life is waiting for me to remember. Life has a broadness, a bigness, an okayness, a calmness, and an ease. There is a steadiness to the universe, and to a certain extent, *choices make themselves* once the information is clear. Once you know or see enough, an option will fall into place. If a selection is unclear, you simply don't make that choice yet until it is absolutely necessary. So, again, there are circumstances where a will is necessary, where something needs to be said or done. But many times, inside our minds, we are creating our urgency. We can learn to stop doing that. We can absolutely learn not to believe the *artificial* deadlines inside our heads.

These "mind deadlines" can be dangerous because when we force an answer into existence, it can go wrong. And so if we take all of that personally, if we make our choices mean something about how good or wise or whatever we are, the danger is that our reactions or responses to anything, any question or problem, can seem to validate those voices in our heads telling us that we're wrong. And, of course, this is an echo of your childhood, like everything in this book. Adults forced you into having answers, and it didn't feel good. They should not have done that to you. Even though it might feel like it, you won't usually "get in trouble" as an adult in the same way you did as a child. When you were a kid, you may have been programmed to avoid getting into trouble no matter what. Some people don't grow out of that. They embrace that avoidance of danger thoroughly and try to become the perfect people pleaser. Or some people rebel against it. They become permanent teenagers who want to defy everyone and everything. But regardless of how you reacted, the chances are that the primary teaching you got was this: You need to make the right decisions. If you don't, you will get in trouble.

And by the way, wrapped up in all of this is the belief that you're supposed to know things you don't know. You're supposed to be a "wise" decision-maker at six years old. You're supposed to see all the consequences of the things you "should have known better" about. "You should have known better" is such an odd thing to try to teach a child, because, even as adults, we can't know better, and we don't.

It's also much more fun, beautiful, and delightful to be alive when you don't carry around the responsibility to "know better." Life is better when we don't feel any obligation to know before we know.

Life is better when we don't feel any obligation to know before we know.

It's true that in some situations you will have experience to draw upon when making choices. But just as often, you try to call up that experience to help you, and fear paralyzes you from using it. Holding on to "should have known better" keeps you busy fearing outcomes instead of listening to your heart. You don't tune in to what you *can* know; you don't see what *is* crystal clear and accurate for you. Fearing that you don't know what you "should" know can become an excuse when you don't want to deal with the consequences of what you actually do know.

For example, let's say you are questioning a job change, saying to yourself, "Should I stay in this position? My boss is abusive, but I enjoy the work." What if you do know the answer? What if your heart *is* aware of what's best? And just to reiterate my earlier point, this is not about being perfect or having the right answer, but the most likely truth is that you do know that you don't deserve abuse in any form and that you'd rather find similar work elsewhere. You do know the healthiest and happiest thing to do. You know what you want and what would be good to happen next—but you're spending your energy finding a way to avoid that truth out of fear. Hiding behind "I don't know" is causing you actual harm, real pain. And it's obfuscating the honest answer for you.

"I don't know." The person you are (or who you become) when you're in that very young-feeling place of believing "I don't know" shrinks you. The you of "I don't know what to do" is not a you filled with self-kindness. It is a you filled with pain for yourself. It's a scary and lonely place, filled with thoughts like, *It's all up to me. I must do it right. I can't do it right. Please leave me alone. I don't know.*

Yeah. If you avoid choosing, you can't make the wrong choice. If that echoes how you often felt as a kid, try this version instead: "I'm going to look clearly;

I'm going to breathe. I'm going to be open to all the information that I have right now. And if there is clarity, if there is a direction that the universe wants to move in, I will be the vehicle for that movement. If there is a clear choice, I will take responsibility for speaking that truth."

You could also say, "If there's no clear choice, I'll wait. And when there is a clear choice, I'll act. I am an adult. I am the person who is willing to set the choice in motion. I vow to stay open and to be as clear as I can be about a choice I need to make." We're talking about taking responsibility. We're talking about not hiding. If you are constantly in a state of "I don't know what to do," you're trying to avoid responsibility for any outcome. But that's not really how it works.

The reason you fall back on "I don't know what to do" when you actually have a lot of clarity is that you're hiding. "I don't know what to do" can be a lie. It's a lie about who you are, and it's a lie about how the universe works. And, of course, it is its own decision. You are putting your thumb on the scale of the universe, giving weight to your incompetence and your own unwillingness to admit that you're worthy and that you—like everyone—deserve to participate fully in society and life.

> **"I don't know what to do" can be a lie.**

Systemic factors play a part in this. Some privileged people make whatever decision they want, seemingly arbitrarily, and just kind of eff around without any consequences at all. As a result, they make pretty constant and enthusiastic mistakes. They harm many people, sometimes effing things up on a global scale, and nothing happens to them.

Meanwhile, you're deeply afraid of what will happen if you spell something wrong in a work email. The other thing we need to address is the matter of proportion. Why are you so special that you deserve the most significant punishment for the slightest mistake?

Why are you so special that you deserve the most significant punishment for the slightest mistake?

If you use "I don't know" as a hiding place, you're not being fair to yourself. You deserve the *freedom* to make a mistake. You deserve the freedom to speak your truth as you see it in one minute, and to see a different truth two minutes later, and then voice that one. I've laid out a formula here: Make a decision once you've waited for clarity to arrive; if a decision must be made, do what seems best and be easy with yourself. If you wait for clarity and it does arrive, have the guts to take responsibility, to be a conduit of the universe's wisdom, and say what your choice is. Then also take responsibility for whatever the fallout is.

You're not going to be good at that process right away. It's going to take practice. And there will be times when you make a decision and it doesn't go over well. In those cases, have the willingness to restate what you see—the clarity you have. I'm talking about a new approach to decision-making, where you're calm, you're seeking, you're noticing. You are looking at a choice without self-judgment and without assuming that you are powerless. You attempt to view your choice without thinking that you are incompetent and that you're "less than," and without considering you don't belong here. And then, you speak the truth if there is truth to be expressed. Your job is to simply voice the decision that has revealed itself when there is such a decision.

Let's Stop and Think for a Moment

Are there other times in your life when you have needed practice? Have you learned a new language or instrument? Did you expect yourself to be perfect right away? How could you be "good" at compassionate decision-making right away, when you were never taught that skill, and you were never shown an example of that skill?

This approach is almost the opposite of how your family likely taught you to make decisions. When you were a kid, you were taught or shown that the choices you make have to be the *right* ones. You had to be perfect to survive. When I was a kid, I had to use my intelligence to be one step ahead of my "caregivers" so that they didn't traumatize or further abuse me. So, for me, decision-making became highly pressurized and highly tied to my safety and worth, and decision-making became incredibly lonely.

Imagine yourself as a kid, all alone. Remember it. You were alone and had to make decisions, and you had been told lies. They told you that making the right decision would get you out of loneliness. If you could be perfect, then you could be embraced. Make the right decisions, and you will be accepted. It's time to put all of that down. You have believed the lies for too long. You thought for years that it was all up to you, and that it had better be right, or you were going to get in trouble—"trouble," in this case, being pure and deserved rejection. Even adequate or well-meaning parents can teach their children to be afraid of decision-making. It's no surprise that anyone would try to hide behind "I don't know" and "I don't know what to do." Not believing in yourself and clinging to "I don't know what to do" is an easy way to opt out.

And right now, life is calling you to opt in. Life wants you to speak its truths. Life wants you to help express its decisions. Life wants you to move forward. Life wants you to be part of the flow, part of the unfolding process, part of the fun. And once decision-making is not about whether you're a good decision-maker, whether you're intelligent enough, or whether you made

Decision-making can even become fun.

the right decision, you're free. Once it's not about your worth, decision-making can even become fun.

We make the best choices we can. We speak the best truths we can. When we see the clarity, will we have the bravery to express the best decisions into existence? That's the place to be in when you decide! That's the place to be. Step forward when life asks you to participate. In Buddhism, there is a concept called the middle way. This idea can be used in decision-making by asking yourself to do anything but the two choices that your brain has offered you. Unfortunately, brains are infamous for always giving us two crappy options. To go back to our earlier example, you may be wondering if you should leave a job or stay in your position. It may seem like a simple either-or choice. Most people state these kinds of decisions like this: "Should I stay in my job that I hate and suffer, or should I leave my job and have no money and be scared and suffer?" Brains, for whatever reason, love to structure life as a constant process of choosing between two suffering-infused and horrid choices.

Your brain is wired to funnel a decision into two choices. And also, your brain will almost always frame the two choices. So, the concept of the Buddhist middle way isn't to pick the thing that's "best" between your two bad decisions; it's to choose any third choice. Just pick anything. This choice may be in the middle, between the two options your brain presents, or it may be in a surprising place somewhere else. Your brain has told you that you must suffer with choice A *or* suffer with choice B. What's the answer? Make a nonbinary choice. Make a holistic, informed selection. Do something outside the box of your mind. Unhappy in your job, but worried about leaving? Maybe the middle way is to make a change at work to improve your situation. Find that other option and speak that into existence. You must practice seeing the biggest, broadest, most open possibilities of a situation. And above all, give yourself the gift of not having to get it right. Even the choices of "right" and "wrong" are often used against us by our own outlook. Your brain will use right and wrong as two hard classifications to create impossible standards for you. Life is often very complicated, and this black-and-white thinking is harmful.

Make a nonbinary choice.

Once you let yourself off the hook, broaden your mind into seeing more than two stark options, and allow yourself to search for the clarity you know is there—you will find a wave of deep peace. Sometimes life clarifies something for us, and we don't realize it at the time. Sometimes clarity comes rushing in with such force that nuance is swept away, and our lives change instantly. Sometimes clarity looks horrid to anyone outside, but we grow and thrive because the truth shines within us.

Unfiltered Real Life

I've been sitting here in my apartment, letting the subject of this chapter settle in my heart. I've been breathing and surrounding myself with love, as I often do, just being kind to myself and saying kind things to myself within my mind. And I realized that I was feeling stuck about this subject in particular, and the opportunity to talk about it to you was too delicious to pass up because my brain was doing exactly the thing I warn against in this chapter. I was given two bad choices by my brain. Choice one, skip writing this; I was feeling stuck. I could simply forget about it and move on. There was a lot of suffering in that choice because I think the subject of making decisions and how we make them is vital. And I work with so many people who suffer and agonize over making decisions—how they should make them, how they should feel about them, and what they mean. And the other choice my brain offered, choice two, was to force myself to produce a chapter that wasn't ready—that my soul hadn't entirely formed or formulated. So, neither choice is a good choice!

To pull back the curtain a little bit on book writing, it's essential to just put the words on the page. You have to produce what we call a terrible first draft. Then you can shape it and form it and, well, mold the clay of the words into what you'd finally like.

That's a good method, but I also choose my subject matter carefully, and I want to connect with you on a genuine level. So, throwing out a quick draft didn't feel right. But I also realized I wanted to show some of the unformed draft of *me*, some of the unfiltered *real life* of who I am. I've encountered many teachers, authors, and guru types who pretend to be fully formed and perfect. And I don't think that model of teaching is beneficial. So, as often as I can, I like to show that I live this stuff. I sit with these ideas. For example, I wait for clarity.

So here's the clarity that has come to me. The most important thing I can impart to you is that I care. I care about you. I care that you won't have to live in a world in which your decisions define who you are, or your choices automatically define your soul, or right and wrong define your personhood. I don't want you to live in that world. I don't want *you* to live like that. Part of the formula that may not make sense to you yet is that mistakes were stolen from you when you were a child.

You weren't permitted to make mistakes. In fact, it goes beyond permission. Your parents took mistakes off your menu of choices. They took mistakes out of the equation for you. Sometimes when I coach people one on one, I will tell them to go make a mistake, as homework. I tell them to make a mistake consciously. They get so afraid. We all get so fearful about making the wrong choices. I tell them, "Please make a mistake and love yourself through it. Please choose a mistake that's very low stakes. Choose something that's very far down on the consequences list. Choose something that's not going to affect you too negatively. Choose something that will not affect the world too negatively, and purposefully decide to do it the wrong way. Purposefully choose to make a mistake."

Practice making a mistake and having it not mean you're a bad person.

When I assign that to people, they tend to get very anxious. They tend to get very upset, and we purposefully start with something low stakes because what we're practicing is a process. The process is about folding the possibility of making a mistake back into your life. My wish for you is to experience something in a way you didn't anticipate, to experience something that you were conditioned to believe would make you a bad person, to allow the screaming voices in your brain to "prove" you are incompetent or wrong or bad—and to simply continue. Do the next thing. Practice making a mistake and having it not mean you're a bad person.

And tell yourself kind things like I was sitting here telling myself as I tried to write this chapter. I felt stuck because I was trying to do this chapter "effectively" or "right" or "in the best way." But I realized what I want to do is cut right to the heart of

There is no such thing as an outcome that means you are deficient.

the matter and tell you what might be the most important thing for you to learn: There is no such thing as an outcome that means you are deficient. There is no such thing as an outcome that means you are unworthy. There's no such thing as a place you can get to, a thing you can produce, a thing you can say, anything that happens along the timeline of your life, that means something about your worth.

As we discussed earlier, that's what the middle way promises. The middle way promises that you can find another option that is compassionate for all. But it is also an option that breaks the matrix of right/wrong, good/lousy, mistake/success. The middle way is the decision that breaks how you were told decisions work. You can come to a decision without a sense of right or wrong. You can come to a feeling of peace around a subject, decision, interaction, or email without it having to be correct, exemplary, or perfect. And as a matter of fact, you might find the ultimate peace without even knowing an answer. You may find an ultimate peace beyond fear, where every part of your life is simply okay. You can craft a life filled with love in all of its aspects.

And if you fill your life with love, a decision *still* might not be clear. We aren't psychic. We aren't masters of the future. There are times when no decision is the decision. There are times when we wait and support ourselves in the pain of waiting.

Let's Stop and Think for a Moment

Where will you purposefully choose the middle way? Is there a part of your life today where it seems that you only have two "bad" choices? Will you strive for the third or middle choice? Will you do something unexpected? Here's a hint: Look for a choice that's compassionate to everyone involved, including you.

It's Never Too Late to Do Nothing

Let's take an extremely subtle look at this process of waiting for information from life. It's time to take "I don't know" a step further. We have covered a few very important points about decision-making. It's okay not to know what to do. It's okay to step into the flow of life, look to your own experience, and stop hiding behind how you're expected to act. You've learned how to make decisions and to stay with yourself, on your side, and you know that it's okay to support yourself from beginning to end in any decision-making process.

So now, I'd like to tell you about a principle I learned at the monastery that deeply and profoundly changed my life: It's never too late to do nothing. One of the cornerstone elements most of us feel around decision-making is urgency, and it's almost always a false urgency. I get very fond of returning, again and again, to not deciding before it's time, and to not respond, not jump in, and to let things rest if they would like to rest. It's one of the most complex skills to learn. As a kid, society taught us to take the events of our lives personally.

You deserve a life where you have enough freedom to wait when waiting is appropriate. You deserve the liberty to wait for clarity when that's appropriate. And you deserve the freedom to step in, speak up, and tell the truth when that is the thing to do. Remember that it's never too late to do nothing the next time things feel urgent.

Are the stakes as high as my brain tells me they are?

So, if you think your circumstances are pressuring you into making a decision, and the decision is simply not clear, take a deep breath, do your best to be kind to yourself, and look squarely at whatever the question is. Does this decision have to be made right now, right this instant? Are the stakes as high as my brain tells me they are? Are things as urgent as I believe?

I hope you'll get to know through trying this out that there are so many times when we can just breathe, be still, and let decisions go for a while. That's how change happens. That's, perhaps ironically, the space from which clarity happens. I think that phrase "It's never too late to do nothing" is just pointing us to a way of life, reminding us that we have the option to wait. We always want the most enormous perspective of any situation possible. We need space to be able to do that. We can practice seeing a situation from as many nonurgent angles as possible. Allow yourself that space. I know we talked a little bit about how claiming "I don't know" can be a kind of decision. But this is different—more subtle. You can create a space within where "I don't know" isn't a problem. That's how you discover that there is a lot you do know. I'm talking about giving yourself the time and peace to see clearly, to trust the wisdom you already have, to move forward in the way of clarity when it is time to do so. The clarity will guide you. And it's a heck of a peaceful way to live. And honestly, we all deserve that peace, especially as kids.

KEY TAKEAWAYS

1. Be mindful of artificial deadlines. Answers that we force into existence are rarely the correct ones.

2. You already have the instincts to make the most critical decisions in your life. Follow and trust your heart. You give the best advice, after all.

3. If your heart is unsure, wait for clarity or find an unexpected "rule-breaking" middle way.

4. It's never too late to do nothing.

Dear Little Jeffrey, Age Six

I know you love the sound of the dishwasher. I know you love to stretch your fingers wide on the front surface and feel the vibrations through your palms—you're fascinated and enjoying its sensation. It'll take you years to realize that you love the sound and the running and the vibrations of the dishwasher because to you, it all means that Mom is in a good mood. It means that everything is in its place. It means that she has had enough time and enough relief to load the dishwasher. It was rare that she was somehow stress-free enough to pour the powdery soap into the small compartment, close the door, and switch it on. The vibrating sloshes meant safety. And the sound will mean security to you for many, many years. You are so beautiful, Little Jeffrey. And you are so sure of yourself. Nowadays I get asked, "What advice would you give to your six-year-old self?" I always answer the same way. I wouldn't give you any advice. But there is one thing I want to tell you, six-year-old Jeffrey. I want to say thank you. Thank you for holding on to who we are. Thank you for carrying the memory of what it's like to be running around, rambunctious, free, and happy.

You're full of yourself in the best way. You're on the cusp, but you haven't yet learned you have to carry around a "good reason" just for existing. Instead, you understand yourself and your world with easy freedom. And although I regained some of that freedom for myself today, it will never be as pure as it is for you.

You will go on a journey for many years, trying to cover up who we are. You will try to hide yourself and deflect attention away from the simple and small and beautiful truth that you embody with such gusto. You are a fine, fantastic, femme child. You are an authority on fun. You sparkle, and I love every bit of you. You don't yet understand why boldly saying, "I like Barbies!" can stop a room full of adults dead in their tracks. You don't yet know why they think your authority and experience are "wrong." Years from now, the memory of who you are and the sparkle that you have, the joy that you bring, and the twirling essence that you embody will help to unlock a lot of pleasure for us. You will allow us to speak our truth. Thank you for being the librarian of that truth and the archivist of our freedom. Thank you for being so sure. Thank you for dancing. Thank you for loving and thank you for having a lot of joy.

Part of your beauty is that you smile. Part of your beauty is that you walk on the balls of your feet. Little spiritual high heels, lifting you toward the sky. And part of your beauty is that you laugh. Sadly, though, I know that you are already gathering the bricks that you will place one by one into our wall of protection. They are starting to weigh you down. But right now, before you build our wall, I must tell you that you are so precious to me. You haven't yet learned to filter your words or essence—at least not too much. But your quality of ease around speaking the ultimate truth will inspire me later. I think you may not even know what a mistake is yet. And bless you! I'll try to return to that version of not knowing as soon as possible.

And you're already so bright! You embody the intelligence that animates the whole universe. You are a beautiful child who can speak with the adults and feel with the adults. Adults tell you often that you're mature for your age. At six years old. I will realize, many years later, that this means we were growing up a little too fast. And our chance to be a free kid was quickly being stolen from us. Remember that most adults don't "know better" about who you are or where your heart is. So, together, let's find a way to play more. Let's find ways to be immature for our age! I know you've memorized a lot of Bible verses. I know you've tried to seem like the perfect Christian so that others won't make fun of you. You're already starting to say things in particular ways so people won't "suspect" you. And so they won't reject you. It's terrible that people are so cruel.

I'm so sad that you've already begun to feel alone and isolated. It's not fair that you've started to compensate for something so beautiful in you. Your rainbow LGBTQ essence is maybe the most beautiful thing about you, and the fact that you feel the need to diminish that essence in order to survive is depressing to me. You are a gorgeously emotional, beautiful child. I'm incredibly delighted that you have the wisdom and the gravity of someone who has already experienced so much. But I want to let you know that you don't have to grow into someone who is so heavy. If I were there with you, I would buy you a Barbie. I would buy you several Barbies. I would purchase you the Barbie patio play set because I know you've wanted it for months and months and months. I know you feel like Barbie yourself. And I know that in your room, late at night, when everybody else has gone to bed, you pretend to be Barbie. You pretend to be Bette Midler. You pretend to be Julie Andrews. I can see you in my mind's eye.

Late at night, you are filling Mom's old pantyhose with rice and putting two rice-filled pantyhose feet into a bra that you stole from your sister. When you wear that bra, you feel happy. You feel free and fun and gorgeous. In your sister's old dress, you beautifully shine. Hold on to that feeling. That feeling is a deep knowledge about yourself and your direction in life. Whenever you don't know what to do, you can return to that feeling and ask your heart for advice. And, of course, it's never too late to do nothing. Just come back to that feeling. Remember it: ten thirty at night, in the middle of winter, with condensation on the corners of the old farmhouse windows—the stars outside cut through the crisp night air. And the joy you feel in your dress cuts

Whenever you don't know what to do, you can return to that feeling and ask your heart for advice.

*through your already-secretive life. Your happiness will in-
spire me for years to come. I will remember. Your twirling
will make me happy for the rest of my life.*

*After we're all grown up, I'll make videos dedicated to
you. I'll be playing in our barn still. I'll make videos
where we twirl and sing and run around looking pretty.
And it will all take me back to memories of you and your
time in the farmhouse. You bring me such joy. I know it's
hard for you to make friends. I see a lot of people make
fun of you. But your resilience and your ability to survive
such loneliness are incredibly inspiring to me. I know you
play in the woods a lot. I know you run around with trees
for friends, confessing to bug confidants. The animals in
the forest around the farm don't make fun of you, and
they don't judge you for having a lisp or being so beautifully feminine.*

*It seems to me that the earth and the forest understand
you. Your gender, femme-ness, and beauty are all so natural. You can be your confident self around them. Feminin-
ity flows from you so bountifully. Yet, even at such a
young age, you're already learning to hide that femme side
of you. You're slipping from confident and accepting into
darkness. I'm sad that you're learning to be afraid that
your father or mother will "catch" you being you.*

*But I wanted to tell you something fundamental. It's
going to take a while, but I'm going to give you freedom
years from now. After we're grown, I'm going to parent
you again. I'm going to provide you with the childhood
that you always deserved. I'm going to give you a free*

re-childhood, where you get to wear what you want. With me, you can say what you want, play with what you want, and dance around whenever you want. I will help you put down the baggage of what you're already learning about hiding who you are. I hope that I can do a good job and help you learn to be free. You, in your beauty, in your wonderfulness, will help me as an adult. You will help me remember to be free. You're going to help me be like a kid again and have fun in my life.

That is a beautiful gift for which I can never repay you. I hope that you can feel me and how much I admire you even now as you sit with your hands on the dishwasher. With tears in my eyes, I just wish you could feel the love I am sending you right now, thirty-eight years later. I wish you peace across time and space. Thank you for learning how to survive. I guess it goes without saying, but I wouldn't be here without you and how you're already learning how to compensate for that beautiful queerness. And without your shining example, I wouldn't be able to stop caring so much about what other people think of me. I wouldn't be able to twirl and be unrestrained as an adult. Without you, I wouldn't feel whole. And honestly, I wouldn't feel happy. You are the essence of authenticity. You are the essence of floating freedom. Thank you! You have such confidence, and it's because you fully accept yourself!

I wish your school and your church wouldn't take your freedom away from you. I want the monstrous self-talk not to become a habit. I feel like pleading, "Please don't *let anyone train you to talk down to yourself." But of course, it has to be that way if we're going to survive. You need to be what your parents want for at least a few years, so that you can eat, so that you can have (a warped version of) love, so that we can survive. You are already starting to "inner police" yourself with words, and there is no way to stop it. I know that things are already feeling dark, and it breaks my heart. Your lightness is the most essential thing in our lives. And it is slipping under the mask called "the perfect child." Would you do me a favor? Would you play a little bit extra for me? Would you put on a dress and twirl a little more for me? Would you continue to be full of yourself and your heart for just a little while longer? Would you soak up that feeling of knowing what to do and who you are? Please?*

Are you aware that you know a lot more than many adults around you? Are you aware that you understand how life works, how gender works, and how the human spirit works more than some grown-ups do? It's no coincidence that people at church already see you as a spiritual leader. It's no wonder that you get asked to read the scripture and testify in church, even at such a young age. You are divine. I know it's ironic. I know you already feel like the people at church don't love you because of who you are. I know you already feel like the people at church might reject you if they knew all there is to know about you. But you are divine. No one can take that from us. I'm sorry that I will take it away from myself for a few years.

But you will help me find it again! You are the true spirit and the true meaning of the divine. I love you for that especially. In the next few years, I'll become more and more unsure. Things will get shaky, and life won't be this clear and innocent again for many years. But you are at the beginning of a beautiful journey. You are the first bookend. You are the sure, beautiful, spiritual bookend in a lifetime of reconnecting. You are the pure feeling of freedom and fun that will take me years to refind. But when I do find it again, I will think of you, and I will be so grateful for your beautiful innocence and your free, wild, and tremendous heart.

In your journal or on some fancy paper, write your own letter to your six-year-old self. What would you have wanted to hear back then? Imagine yourself at that age. Where were you? How did you feel day to day? Can you give your young self a pep talk? Can you say "thank you"? As you write your letter, set aside any impulse to treat your young self the way adults treated you then.

Part 2

Change Your Dynamic with Others

You are your most important relationship. But (sometimes unfortunately) we inhabit various communities throughout our lives. We live in a world with . . . others. And while it may be true that the people who surround us are reflections of us in some way, other people are unpredictable reflections! Other people are frustrating and scary and difficult and wonderful and distracting and fun.

You can learn to stay with yourself no matter what other people bring into your life. In fact, you can learn to thrive with a deep sense of belonging. You can actively create places where you feel at home and you can give up on what other people think of you for good. One helpful step in your path toward a sense of justice and peace will be to thoroughly and enthusiastically celebrate your anger. Yes, I said anger. Your anger can guide you to a sustained feeling of ultimate justice. In the next few chapters, I will show you how to be an angry-happy, peaceful-caring warrior who isn't fazed by what others think of you.

Chapter 4

Stop Trying to Belong and Start Creating the Spaces You Want to Belong To

Getting Married, on Zoom

I never thought I would get married. My husband, Jeff, and I have talked many, many times about how it never even occurred to us growing up. I thought marriages were for straight people. Having a marriage ceremony is for a cisgender couple—a man and a woman. At every wedding, there's the dress. There's the tux. And we know who's wearing each. There's lots of extravagances. Gifts that people may not even need. Oh yes, and lots of food. But growing up, neither Jeff nor I ever thought that a wedding could be on the horizon for us. I remember thinking I *could* date, and I felt it would be delightful to have a fictitious boyfriend finally swoop in and accept me for who I am and rescue me from my terrible childhood. I waited for years and years to find a Prince Charming who could erase all the trauma and awfulness that had been hallmarks of my life so far. I've talked a little bit about how Jeff and I met and how I've worked to maintain our relationship. (I'm glad he's in my life!) He's still here, married to me, even though everything in me was screaming to kick him out of my life when we first started dating. I'm not proud of it, but in the beginning, everything in me tried to get away from him as fast as I could. Back then, I was still working on what my personal, authentic needs were. I was still growing and learning about myself, and I thought I didn't deserve or fit with someone as wonderful as Jeff.

I've never told the story of how we ended up getting married. Marriage seemed like an institution that I never could belong to when I was a kid, and it wasn't even legal. The government also didn't recognize non-binary people like me when I was young. Then, when I was an adult, gay marriage became legal. But it still didn't feel like it was all that inclusive. The movement centered around specific kinds of gay marriages—a particular image. And so, for many years, both Jeff and I felt like we were committed to each other and loved each other very deeply, and the idea of marriage didn't enter our minds. Then one day it occurred to me that we could get married our way—that we didn't have to imitate anyone else to have a valid and lasting marriage.

So, I decided to pop the question. We had this weird tradition in our relationship. Well, not weird, actually, just an unconventional and yet poetically beautiful tradition. For our first anniversary, I gave Jeff a jar with little slips of paper inside. Each paper had something I loved about him written on it. For one month, he was supposed to pick out a message every day and read it (and treasure it and cherish it). Pretty romantic, right? Well, guess what? I wanted to overachieve our love. I needed to show extra-credit affection. I'm that kind of person. I'm also sneaky. So, behind Jeff's back, I put more slips of paper in that jar. I just kept writing and sticking notes in the jar so that what was supposed to be a month-long gift went on and on—a Hanukkah oil lamp of romance.

By the way, could you tell I was poor at the time? And thank goodness for that, because we both enjoy the memory of that jar. We still have that jar and the slips of paper to help us remember. Because I couldn't buy him extravagant things, I gave him a vessel with compliments, and the vessel magically grew and became bottomless, boundless, endless.

The bits of gratitude on paper said the loveliest things: "You accept me for who I am." "You come to see me when I'm in a play." Like our love, those slips of paper just kept growing and growing. And six months went by, a year went by, and eventually, we decided to morph that gift into texting each other every night. Still to this day, before bed, we text each other five things we love about the other person. Even if we've had a disagreement or are away from each other, we still text like clockwork.

I proposed to Jeff back when I was still using paper. I decided to give him an extraordinary little paper strip before an upcoming trip. He was traveling to Italy for work, and I was going with him. Italy is one of his favorite places because he wrote his master's thesis on Caravaggio (he's a smarty-pants). And Jeff specifically wrote about the queer aspects of Caravaggio's sexuality, which flourished in Rome. So that city means a lot to him. I knew we would be going to see some of his favorite Caravaggio paintings in some of his most beloved Roman churches. So, I wrote one more message for the jar: "Will you marry me?" (I was being very romantic about this!)

I wanted him to pick it out of the jar before we left for Italy, and we could celebrate as fiancés. The only problem was a week went by . . . two weeks went by. He didn't pick that piece of paper. It felt like, day after day, he picked every *other* paper out of that little container. And I was wondering how to encourage him to pick that one, you know, like a magic trick or something. I thought about replacing all the paper slips with ones that said, "Will you marry me?" But instead, eventually, I decided to take that slip of paper to Rome with us. I figured the universe was trying to tell me something: "Propose in Rome. It will be romantic." And there we were, in a Roman church in front of a beautiful Caravaggio painting called *The Conversion of Saint Paul.* The painting depicts a conversion in the biblical sense: A man named Saul goes from being an unbeliever to believing with his whole heart. The focus of the painting is, actually, a beautiful horse's hind end. The horse's rider (Saul) has been thrown to the ground, stunned. The fall has awakened Saul. In fact, in a moment of clarity, Saul has become Paul. Like a trans person, Paul has been thrust by stunning clarity out of a deadname and into a significant life change. As we stood there, taking in the painting, I said, "I have a gift for you." It was a necktie from his favorite clothing brand. Stuck inside the necktie was that slip of paper. He took out the tie. The light in his eyes was beautiful. He went to put the gift and box away into his bag. I said, "Why don't you try your new tie? Maybe try it on?" Then he saw the paper. He read it. My heart was thumping! He said yes, and we kissed in front of a painted horse. And at that moment, we were engaged. Were we both crying? *Maybe.*

Then we waited a few years! Like many couples, it was a long time before we married. Part of the reason for that was that I was having issues with my family. I didn't know if, deep down in my heart, I wanted my family to be at my wedding. Oh, and it was also because weddings are expensive. We didn't have enough money even to have a *less expensive* wedding. And our families didn't have a lot of money. But maybe the most important reason was that the thought of a conventional wedding just didn't sit right with either of us. We wanted something simpler— something truer to us. When we were living in New York, a few years after my proposal and a few months into the pandemic of 2020, I got an idea. The governor had okayed getting married by Zoom, and that felt right. I had already lived so much of my life online, from Vine to Twitter to Instagram. I thought nothing could be better, more appropriate, or more beautiful. If we got married in the heart of our relationship, in the comforting surroundings of our beautiful home together, it would resonate with both of us. We loved our New York City flat. Since our New York apartment was the first one we had shared, we had so many memories of so many gorgeous times together. On that Zoom were Jeff and I in our apartment, our dear friend Laura in her apartment, and the officiant in a Zoom square all by herself.

And I felt so happy. I finally felt like I belonged at a wedding. It was because it was *just us*. It was one of the most beautiful days of my life. And I want that belonging for you. I want to belong with you. I want you to avoid the pitfalls of "feeling like I don't belong," and I want your focus to shift toward giving yourself a safe space.

Creating Your Own Space

I want you to know that you do belong. I'm very grateful for you. I know that you've probably been lonely for a long time, and it may seem like your loneliness is never-ending. I know that finding your place is significant to you. Well, if you'd like it, you have a home here. You have a family with me.

Shift your focus. In this chapter, we will learn how to go from wanting to belong—from requiring belonging from other people—to creating the belonging you want. To get there, you will have to start creating spaces that will give you what you need. And then you'll be spending time in the rooms you love instead of waiting for and begging other people to recognize you, validate you, include you, or value you. You will also have to learn to make the opportunities you want. This approach is not about "manifesting" or controlling outcomes. And it is not "make your own opportunities" as shorthand for transcending the systemic discrimination you face. This chapter isn't about your "character" giving you the opportunities you wish the world could give you. This advice is not about pressuring yourself to create the impossible. What we *are* talking about is celebrating and concentrating on what is possible in a way that will help you feel like you belong. It may look a heck of a lot like the things you've always wanted, in the end. It might eventually look like the places you've always wanted to be.

So I sat down to write this chapter, and the overwhelming voice in my head, the voice that came from my parents, was saying, *How dare you speak? How dare you tell people to create the spaces where they want to belong? What do you know about it?* And on and on. Sometimes spiritual practice is about not allowing those limiting voices to take residence in your head. Or, to put it more precisely, spiritual practice looks more like having those voices and proceeding anyway. We can all have limiting voices or mean voices in our head, and recognize those voices for what they are (powerless) and proceed anyway.

That primarily is what this chapter is attempting to tell you—to stop listening to those limiting voices, and to stop allowing outside forces to influence your sense of belonging.

A few years ago, I received a very memorable threat. A particularly awful *death* threat. It was years before the threats I received from being "featured" on *Tucker Carlson*. It was 2013, back when I was famous on Vine, and someone got very, very particular, enthusiastic, and hateful in a series of comments. This person told me exactly how they would find me, how they would kill me, the method they would use, where it would happen, what would happen next, and why I deserved it. They went on and on and on and it was very, very detailed.

It wasn't the first time, and you know from my Tucker Carlson story that it wouldn't be the last. But this threat will always stick out, mainly because of how enthusiastically this person depicted their detailed plan. And it will always stick with me as another choice point. I was in a position where I needed to decide if I was going to get up the next day and post. I needed to decide whether having that energy in my life—if receiving death threats—was worth it. Did the hate outweigh the joy of community and the sense of connecting with people that Vine brought me? Did hate overshadow the visibility and attention for my mission that I was able to garner as somebody on social media? The other thing I was considering at the time was, did I want the people who followed me to see me getting death threats in my comments every day? Did I want young people to see an LGBTQ person constantly hated? Eventually, I decided that I would keep posting, and I decided that for a specific reason. The way I felt about posting, the community that grew out of the work I was doing, and the new family that came from it were all worth it. And I felt that the beautiful, loving, and spiritual things that I posted were worth sharing and worth getting death threats over. But also, I wanted to keep posting, and I wanted people (especially young LGBTQ people) to see the negativity that came my way because of it, and then see that I would post again. I was hoping to be an example of receiving a ton of hate and rising again to keep going against all odds.

So I posted the next day and the day after that. No matter what negativity came at me, no matter what threats came at me, no matter what judgments or awfulness came my way, I kept posting. I stuck with the mission, stuck with the love, stuck with the kindness. That was most important to me. And I eventually realized that this is one of the true hallmarks of belonging. No matter what comes your way, you can assume that you belong. No matter what comes your way, you believe that you have every right to be where you are. No matter what comes your way, you have every right to speak up. Making that assumption into a habit didn't happen

No matter what comes your way, you can assume that you belong.

overnight. So, how did I get there? It took a long, long time of practicing, telling myself, "I'm glad you're here." Even still to this day, I will say to my-self, "Thank you, Jeffrey. I'm glad you're here. I love you very much."

And that kind of regular self-talk helps me to remember where I started. All of us need to remember that, generally speaking, babies know they belong. When you first entered this world, you belonged. Babies don't know anything else. We come from this world. We're part of this world. We are the embodiment of belonging in this world. We do have a place. But something happened to many of us, something that our childhood taught us: that we don't belong here, that there's something wrong with us. Eventually, we learn that we need to *strive to belong*. Our parents told us a lie that we need to *prove that we belong*. We got the message growing up that belonging is not our birthright. So we set out on a path of trying to belong, but it doesn't work. And the reason it doesn't work is that we belong already. You can't fix what no one broke.

Many of us have barriers to feeling our belonging. Society has marginalized many of us in various ways. Our world isn't always a just one, and I'm not suggesting that you will be able to give yourself every opportunity that you would like.

There are some things that will be impossible to transcend. Chances are, you will never be able to belong in specific ways. You may never belong at certain religious institutions or in certain schools or workplaces. But as far as belonging here on earth, as far as spiritual belonging, as far as giving yourself the freedom to relax, because you don't have to prove that you belong anymore, all of that is possible. What I am suggesting is that the validation and the belonging and the adoration that you might be craving, if only someone else would give you a chance, could happen to you, whether someone gives you that chance or not.

I'll give you an example. I'm nonbinary. You might say I'm very, very LGBTQ. Yet there aren't any roles for me in musical theater, even though I majored in musical theater in college. You'd think that the theater would be a haven for people like me, but there are almost no roles written specifically for nonbinary performers. And so what I've done is sing and dance my heart out on TikTok. I wanted to give myself an action, a step forward, saying, "Hey, I know I belong. Even if the theater world (ironically!) can't comprehend me, I understand myself. I love that I belong here. And I'm going to *cast myself* in this TikTok. I will put on my heels, put on my sparkly dress, and sing at the top of my lungs. I choose myself."

The thing is, you deserve every chance to belong. You deserve to be part of the group. And if you can step forward and begin to create spaces of belonging, those spaces will be where you belong. On a practical level, this could look like starting a group for you and others around an activity that you love. Go ahead, start a knitting circle or a meditation group. Or perhaps you begin a project with like-minded people who support the causes of justice you care about. Find an excuse—any excuse—to be spending time with people who want what you want and who care about what you care about.

Perhaps it's not fair. But it's also unfair to waste another second trying to belong where you aren't wanted or can't be celebrated. Those spaces that you will create yourself will be the place where you will feel a deep sense of belonging. It's what I've done on social media. I decided to step forward and create the *family* I wanted to belong to. When I was a little kid dancing around in gowns, singing, and having fun, I imagined a loving family. I was putting on plays in the barn, and I imagined being surrounded by people, surrounded by an audience. All those people (my imaginary audience) loved me, accepted me, and found me beautiful. I created light in a very dark childhood. And that lightness has returned through social media.

Despite the negative parts that come with social media, it's through social media that I found the connection, the family, the unconditional love that I was craving when I was a little kid on the farm. And again, I don't want to say that this is manifesting or that I consciously created a new family. The only thing I created was the place where I wanted to belong. I posted about it. I decided a long time ago that I was going to stop waiting for someone else to create my community. I was going to do it myself.

It's why stepping forward, volunteering, and saying yes in all the groups of your life is so important. Every group should be inviting people to become leaders, inviting people to be the progenitors, the creators, and the ones who decide what happens next. All groups should invite people to be not just a group member, but a decision-maker, to be intimately involved and a driving force in the group. It just occurred to me that you (you reading right now) deserve this. It occurred to me that a little part of you, who was trying so hard to belong, earned a place of utter belonging. This idea of finding where one belongs is maybe the most profound human need we have. And one of the paths to belonging is to create the spaces for yourself. You can do it with friends; I'm not saying you have to do it alone. But do find ways within the skills you have and within the opportunities you have to give yourself that belonging in any way you can.

Give yourself that promotion. Become a leader. There is one tricky part to consider, though. When you choose yourself in belonging, it may not feel good at first. You may be so utterly used to not belonging that *not belonging* feels like you. Stick with it, though. This feeling of "belonging isn't me" lessens over time, and eventually, if you give belonging to yourself, you will make spaces that feel authentically filled with unconditional love. And if you are the creator, those spaces can be what you love and want.

And an important point—you should act now. Waiting for other people to give you a sense of belonging is a passive response, but creating the communities yourself is active. It's time to take charge. With this mindset, you know you're going to make the space you want to belong to no matter what happens next, whether it's a success or not. Do that, commit to that, say to yourself, "I'm going to create this space as a place of action." Stop waiting and start doing.

I know it may not seem like it, but this really is a possibility for you in your life right now, even within the chances you have been given. Before you move forward, you should carefully consider the life you want and the life you want to belong to. How can you do the fulfilling activities, how can you live the beautiful dreams, and how can you find belonging and provide the opportunities you want? How can you cast and hire yourself for the perfect part, and how can you find the space to praise yourself? It's about working within the life you have to get what you want. Make a video. Write a play. Apply for that dream job. Get used to making choices that move the ball forward without having to rely on anyone else to get going. Put almost all of your focus there, and your life will become quite different. Who you are and how you move in the world will not be the same. And I will tell you from personal experience that this has become a total guiding force for me.

Perhaps most importantly, for me on my journey, whether I'm writing, coaching, or working on TV projects, anything that I'm acting on, I'm doing to create that sense of belonging, that place where people can belong and participate and have a voice and be valued. I am always trying to create those places. So my secret confession is . . . I'm selfish. I create spaces for belonging for my community, but they're also the spaces I've always wanted. I create spaces where I can feel like I am healing. I crave to feel like I am part of something.

The spaces you're going to create will automatically be significant to you, and probably to others. If I'm not careful, I'll always be trying to prove I belong. So I've decided to focus on creating instead of the feeling of wanting to belong. I got programming as a kid that I don't belong here. And I'm still trying to overcome that. Trying to prove your worth can put you in a very lonely place. When you're in that place, you get trapped in a cycle of trying to work out how to change the way you feel and trying to change how other people think of you. But if you take steps to devote yourself to carving out your own space to belong in, if you focus on creating an ample, broad, loving space, you will finally get the sense of community you've been craving. Your new bellwether will become finding the ways of outwardly expressing your love. And love creates belonging in surprising places and in ways we never expect. I promise you that the spaces you build will reflect light right back to you.

Waiting for Your Safe Space, aka the Spiritual Danger Zone

It's worth giving some thought to how belonging feels. And I mean how it feels in your body to belong. Let's do an exercise together. Stop reading, stick your finger in this page, and *feel* belonging. Close the book. Close your eyes. Take a couple of breaths and feel belonging in your body.

Let's Stop and Think for a Moment

Remember a time when you belonged. What is the experience of that memory? How does belonging feel? Write out what you remember about belonging. Where was it? How old were you? Explore what that memory feels like. Write down the specific places in your body where memory lives. How does it feel emotionally and physically?

Does belonging live somewhere in your chest? Or your shoulders? Or is it an overall feeling of the ability to relax? Does it feel like the chance to let go? The physical feelings around belonging are so important and necessary to explore, because if you're aware of the physical sensations, you can practice going around every day, allowing yourself to feel that way. You can remind yourself to experience your constant belonging, physically. It may not be easy to come back to that feeling. It may take a lot of practice. But whatever the (physical) sense of belonging is for you, why not feel that feeling as often as you can? Why not make a new habit of feeling like you belong?

Why not make a new habit of feeling like you belong?

For many people, their default experience is to enter a space with an assumption that they don't belong. This is the spiritual danger zone. Of course, this comes out of your relationship with your mom and dad (or caregivers). If your parents were abusive, neglectful, or simply incompetent, they instilled a sense that you don't belong. You learned by word or demonstration that you need to be hypervigilant. You need to be hyperaware of everyone and every situation to prove your belonging.

Toxic parents foster an intense need to prove loyalty to the family, to prove that you belong.

Toxic parents foster an intense need to prove loyalty to the family, to prove that you belong. Every day, every situation, can become about proving that you're loyal, proving that you deserve to be in the family. Your parents told you that you don't belong, and so you must confirm you do want to belong "enough" by being 100 percent loyal, even in the face of abuse.

How do parents ask you to do this? They train you to be extra aware of their moods so that you can emotionally support one or both of your parents. With bad parents, you must give them praise. And you must like the right kind of people and dislike the wrong type of people. You prove your belonging to the family by staying loyal to who *we* like and who *we* don't.

I realized after a while that, for my family, my mother acted as a kind of gatekeeper. She would decide who was good and evil on my behalf: who was likable and not, who was a friend, who was a foe—all of it filtered through her. And I was trained to prove that I belonged in the family by agreeing with her assessment. I proved I belong by holding the same opinions as my mom, emotionally supporting her, and holding up her worldview. And I was good at proving that I belonged.

Eventually, I realized that, on a spiritual level, I belonged already. I didn't need to prove that I belong anywhere, or with anyone. And I can create a brand-new family filled with people who don't require that same pledge of loyalty (or, more accurately, subservience). So, to find my own communities, I've always been a person who participates a lot. And when I went to the monastery, I dove into Zen practice with an incredible amount of enthusiasm. I became a star student. I helped other people. I led meditation groups. I became a teacher. I helped other people to have awakenings.

I was able to benefit so much from Zen practice that way. I learned that, by participating, I was able to feel such a sense of belonging. I was so invested in that community because I was helping it thrive. I was helping to develop the community. I was helping others, and it felt good. So, when I left the monastery, I did my best to belong to the world, shifting my focus toward creating a sanctuary here in my "outside" life. I committed myself to create a space of belonging. But I realized belonging could also be a trap.

If you don't do the work to think about what belonging means, it will always be about *other people*. If you're not careful, belonging will always be about (1) helping others feel good or (2) obsessing over whether or not someone else will decide if you belong. What I'm attempting to impart to you is that you can be in the driver's seat of belonging. You can be the one who is speaking up, inviting, and participating at a high level. You can decide that you belong at any time. When you were a kid, you needed to be intelligent. You needed to use your intelligence to make an argument, whether through actions or words, for your worth. You always needed to argue for your belonging.

> **If you don't do the work to think about what belonging means, it will always be about *other people*.**

The time has come to put that intelligence to work on your behalf. You want to shift your focus to using your smarts, ideas, and inspiration to create the community of belonging you have always wanted. It's your only choice. It's your best choice.

And I hope a focus on creating belonging for yourself and others will help you grow into a person who never questions their belonging. It is a great experience to walk into a room and assume you already belong there. I already wrote about the systemic issues earlier in this chapter. And they're real. It seems like there are a lot of spaces out there that the system has designed to be an ill fit for us. But I choose to enter every room assuming that I belong, and it has changed my life. What other people think and what they try to do is almost irrelevant because I am clear within myself. So, yes, there will always be doors closed to me, but there were many more doors open to me than I realized. And there were a lot of doors that I didn't realize I could simply reach out and open for myself. I didn't even know I was learning how to create my community.

I choose to enter every room assuming that I belong, and it has changed my life.

Community Is What You Create

We are all craving community. Now and forever, and that's not a bad thing. I think it's a natural and unavoidable thing. For most of human history, we've lived in tribes, communities, hunter and gatherer bands, societies, and agricultural villages—places where we would wake up each day, interact in the community, then go to bed surrounded by the same people. Without communities, people have a much harder time thriving and even surviving. Humans used to watch the stars with friends and family. For many people, social media has replaced that life. As I write this book, we are in the middle (maybe middle?) of a global pandemic. Many of us are staying at home, working from home, and rarely relating to anyone. And when we do connect with someone, it's only through a screen, and that person may not be a regular friend. On the other hand, we may be connecting to many other people in these one-off social media interactions. It's complicated to have loving, lasting, and beautiful in-person communities during a pandemic. It's nearly impossible. Social media is something I know a bit about, having been a social media star for years now. When I was first famous on the app Vine, it was around 2011. And there were no safeguards. There were no guardrails in the way platforms implement them now. Anyone could say anything. And they did. There wasn't even a system to report people or check in on someone who was being targeted or bullied on a social media app.

And today, even with (rudimentary) safeguards, the danger is still there. There are many people who are extremely cruel online. And if the only spaces, the only sense, the only mimicking of a community you're getting in your life is through social media apps, that might compound your preexisting problems with how you view belonging, or how you view communities. You might start to think that community itself is dangerous and that other people are always extreme. Maybe the pandemic compounded by the cruelty of social media could make you lonely. I can't say this for certain, but I wouldn't doubt that this has led to many people pinning so many of their hopes on finding a romantic partner. Many of us wish for one remarkable person to mirror all that is best in us and share our day. And we want someone to share our deepest, deepest dreams and desires. Sometimes, we want that one person to replace a community for us. And one person isn't the answer. That is simply too big of an expectation for one person to carry. What we really need is an in-person community with many, many friends where we could share ourselves and our lives with others. I think one of the issues here is that most of us rush into romantic partnerships. We're hoping, craving, and yearning for that reflection of the *community*, especially if we never had a sense of belonging or community in our childhood.

Let's Stop and Think for a Moment

It's worth considering now what makes a good community. What, to you, is a good friend? Consider the friendships you've had throughout your life. What to you makes a friendship stronger? What makes some friendships last longer than others? What makes you a good friend to others?

I often get accused of being a cult leader. It's a bizarre accusation. And admittedly, it's a subset of the hate that I receive online. But I get comments, more frequently than you might think, saying, "Are you trying to lead a cult? Are you trying to be another God?" I think there are two reasons for this. Number one: I use some language that people associate with cults. I talk about my online community as family. I mean it sincerely, and I know it can be a loaded word for people, but I hope that we're forging a new kind of family in our online space and our online community. Number two: Something cult leaders are known for is a love bomb. They "bomb" their followers with love and compliments, especially early on in the relationship. I'm guilty of doing that. Cult leaders use love bombs as a technique to get others to let their guards down. And then cult leaders manipulate people or start to be mean or abusive to them to get what they want. Of course, I don't do any of that second part. My kindness is sincere. But cults are an extreme example of how our desperation for (outside) love can make us vulnerable to false love.

The sense of family I get from social media, our community online, is genuine. To me, that's the other, more positive side of social media. The internet can be a place to find a true family. You can consciously use social media to find the people you've always been seeking. At least, that's what I feel I've done. Who makes up the community *you've* been craving? Yes, social media comes with awfulness, and oh yes, you're going to have to weed through a lot. And you're going to have to set boundaries and be specific about what you want. And you're gonna have to do a lot of research. But if you're willing to put in that time and effort, I have found that some of my online family is more real than my genetic family was growing up. To the best of your ability, create and find community. Having a community that loves you is crucial. A sense of community is your birthright. Having that sense of community is something that you deserve.

The reason I wanted to write this chapter is so that you might give some thought to what you love in a community, what you find toxic in a community, what you fear about community, and what you want to create. If you could create anything, what would you make? If you stopped focusing your efforts on trying to be accepted into another community, what kind of community would you create? Here are some ideal community attributes for you to consider when forming your own space to belong. I would guess you want a community accepting of everyone—a community that loves the eccentrics, the artists, the lovers, and the dreamers. I would also imagine you want a community that's not built necessarily around *productivity* or work—you want a community based on who you are, not what you achieve. You want a group where membership is based on human value, not the value of the *work* you can offer. I would imagine you want a community where you can work together to find fulfillment and where the focus will be on having enriching lives and beautifully complex interactions. Maybe people are sometimes annoying, perhaps tricky, but you want trustworthy and loving relationships. I also think that your sense of community could include *consistency*. People who are at a place in their spiritual growth and maturity where they can commit to something and can show up when they've committed to showing up. You want to spend time with people who are in a place where they can be responsible for their own part in the group—so that you don't have to do it for them. I wish you the best. I want you to have a happy and joyous community.

As a trans person, I know what it means to create a safe space within myself. My conception of myself, the self my thoughts honor, is finally a safe playground for me. I'm all grown up in the barn of my mind, and I dance. Many queer lives are a patchwork of expressions. We need to be keenly aware of the patches we've adopted from other people. We need to get skilled in touching the safe part of our spirit that knows and loves who we are. I am not trans for anyone else. My soul is not trans in anyone else's safe space. Like many LGBTQ individuals, I have vowed to create an unshakable community within, and I often spend time creating safe communities outside myself. I recommend you explore this balance for yourself too.

KEY TAKEAWAYS

1. Belonging is taken from us throughout our lives, and it is possible to create space for ourselves.

2. For many people, family is chosen. Find your community and select healthy people to invest your energy and love into.

3. Forget using work or achievements to determine your value. Your humanity is more than enough.

Chapter 5

Stop Trying to Control What Other People Think of You and Start Changing What *You* Think of You

Each chapter of this book has been about how you deserve to unlearn the patterns that are holding you back. Before moving on, it's essential to let go of past behaviors and abandon your deeply ingrained habits. It all has a lot to do with letting go of your outward focus. You made a deal at a very young age—it's a deal made with your family and your community: Abandon yourself thoroughly and devote yourself to pleasing others; only then will you belong. You'll be safe. You made a deal before you even knew you were making it. You couldn't possibly have made a different choice. So, the time has come for you to let go of this deal and be free. Let's go deeper.

The Truth

What if I wrote a chapter in a book and didn't care if anyone liked it? What if I wrote a chapter and didn't care if people thought it was good or bad? What if I simply spoke the truth and devoted my life to giving myself the space to tell more actualities? Some facts are so deep inside me and so urgent to get out that I've stopped caring if anyone gets it or gets me. I want to tell you a deep secret about getting other people to like you, about trying to control what others think of you: It's all a lie. Maybe you knew this. It's a lie on several fronts. First, it's a lie that it's even possible. As we know from experience, you can't act in a way so that 100 percent of people will like you 100 percent of the time. But if you are a people pleaser, if you are still constantly trying to do the impossible, if you are spending most of your time trying to get

If you are spending most of your time trying to get people to like you, *you* are lying.

people to like you, *you* are lying. You are lying to yourself and others. You might even feel deeply compelled to manipulate people into liking you. To be completely honest, that's immoral. You learned people-pleasing for innocent reasons. You needed to please to survive. You needed to please to make it through.

But it's time to move on. Every day that you don't move on is a day when you could have stopped lying. Every day you could have stopped *pleasing* in the way your parents taught you to please is a day you could have stopped manipulating yourself and others—when you could have told your personal, profound, unvarnished truth. You know the truth I mean. It's the one the world needs to hear, the truth deep inside you that you've always kept hidden. And when you hide because you think your truth will lead to rejection, you feel fake and disconnected. Your ultimate truth is the truth you hide because you fear that people will be upset or angry if you tell it.

The People-Pleasing

I learned to people-please enthusiastically. I had to, in order to survive and be safe in the household where I grew up. When I was thirteen or so, I reassured my dad that I liked girls. I had a "girlfriend" in middle school, for heaven's sake! Becky! She had braces! And I asked her out! Dating her would be one of the most traumatizing times in my life (sorry, Becky). But more on that later.

Looking back now, assuring my dad that making out with Becky made me straight seems ridiculous with a capital *R*. But at the time, it was my way of trying to avoid violence. Pretty smart, actually. My parents wanted to get me to be someone other than myself throughout my childhood. And to be frank, they thought if they were "good" parents, they would never raise an LGBTQ child. Growing up on the farm, I was a master manipulator/manipulatress. I was a manipulatrix, talented at soothing other people. I had to learn this quickly, to avoid beatings from my father. Eventually, when I was an adult, my dad said to me, "I'm sorry for your childhood. I'm sorry I treated you the way that I did. And I must be honest with you. I was afraid of what other parents would think of me." Evidently, he was wrapped up in pleasing other people too.

Let's Stop and Think for a Moment

Consider the ways you obsess over pleasing people. Are you always the first to show up and the last to leave? Do you always go the extra mile? Are you the one who bakes three things for the bake sale, then sets up the table, sells the cookies, and cleans up afterward? What would happen if you said no to more people more often?

Faking It for Family

I didn't put all the pieces together until much later in life: There was a massive incentive for me to be one step ahead of my mom and dad, to morph myself into the exact child they wanted at the precise time they wanted it so that I could avoid violence, rejection, and judgment. I don't know if you had this experience, but when I was a young child, I felt that my survival was always at stake. Mom and Dad owned the roof over my head. They had the food and shelter, but in addition to that, they held all the love. They guarded the gateway to the religious community and God. They were my protectors, or they were supposed to be. But I had to earn protection.

And so, my young-person brain, my five-year-old, six-year-old, brain, couldn't conceive of my parents being bad parents. And, of course, I couldn't even think of making a choice not to be in their lives at five years old. I couldn't imagine turning my back on my family or packing my bags and leaving. None of that was on the table. I learned to survive within the family in the best way I could. I put on an emotional mask. I shifted my moods and the way I said things; I tiptoed through the house when needed. I changed the way I played. I changed the way I watched TV. I was always on orange-level alert, constantly aware of my parents' moods and energy. I always knew where they were, emotionally.

The Bigger View

Looking back, I could guess that my mom had many problems of her own. She probably needed emotional support, and she didn't seem to be getting it from any source whatsoever. And in a way, it makes weird logical sense for her to turn to her empathetic, beautiful, kind, innocent, and caring child for that emotional support. But of course, that was unfair to me. I should have had the space to be a kid. Instead, what I learned from supporting her and trying to avoid my dad's violence was an incredible skill of shifting the emotions of others. I learned to please and soothe.

I should be clear. It's not possible to change someone's feelings. We can't ultimately walk someone else's journey, and we can't flip a switch in their emotional state. But what I became was very, very good at cheering someone up, being "emotionally useful," making a good point so that they could see the broadest perspective and maybe have a shift toward feeling better.

Those are all excellent skills—except the reason I was using them was so that everyone I encountered would like me. I hoped that everyone I met would find me *valuable*. I was trying to avoid the violence and rejection of my parents by using those skills with everyone. Here's the ultimate catch, and it's maybe the hardest thing I have to say in this chapter: That made me a liar. And by the way, it also made me incredibly lonely. I was totally without connection and community because I was presenting a false image of myself that I thought was likable and useful. But again, purely and technically, at the heart and root, it also made me a liar. If somebody came to me, a coworker at work, for instance, and they needed feedback, I would lie to (try to) force the person to like me. If a friend needed profound advice about moving on from a bad relationship in their life, I would lie. I would lie so they would like me. I would tell them what I assumed they wanted to hear. And I would never encourage them to look at deeper patterns, or try something different, or change their behavior, because I thought those pills would be too hard to swallow. And I felt that swallowing them would make the other person reject me.

Learning to stop worrying about what other people think of me and to stop trying to control what other people think of me has been a journey of learning to tell the truth. You can tell the whole truth kindly. You can speak truths with integrity and compassion. And oftentimes, a sincere version of the truth is the kindest and most compassionate interaction we can have with others. You don't have to be mean to tell the truth, but you also don't have to worry about being liked. That's not your job. It wasn't my job. When I gave up on it, I began to feel so much better.

Oftentimes, a sincere version of the truth is the kindest and most compassionate interaction we can have with others.

There's another part of this that I would really like you to know: The way to get out of this habit of hiding your truth is to begin to see yourself the way you wish others would see you. I used the phrase "start changing what you think of you" in the title of this chapter because society tells us not to think highly of ourselves. Individualistic American culture can encourage some people to be quite assertive—but only some people. Straight, white, cisgender men are often taught to assume they are the best.

And anyone else is told they mustn't shine very brightly. A lot of us get the constant message, "Don't puff up, don't be full of yourself." Don't see the best in yourself. Don't be proud of yourself for who you are. Essentially, if what you're constantly looking for is a first-place blue ribbon from others, and you think you get your ribbon by presenting to others a false version of yourself, you will always be outwardly focused. If you are constantly becoming what other people want, you will never blossom into the authentic you.

Being Kind to Yourself Instead

If you're doing all that, you should just give the ribbon to yourself. It is entirely possible to list your best qualities repeatedly every day until it sinks in. Then, you can start to fill the void instilled in you by your mom and dad. It's not enough to just stop thinking bad things about yourself. It's not enough to stop walking around with a constant mental stream of negative thoughts about what's wrong with you. It's not even enough to begin to see yourself as worthy and talented and valuable. Those things are great, and should be practiced, but they're not the ultimate fulfillment of what you deserve. You must *act* to make your realizations real and change your habits. You must act out the truth to solidify the truth for yourself. It's important to consciously practice embodying your best qualities fairly and honestly. And you need to do that without worrying about what other people will think. Here's a tip: Speak plainly and clearly (and often!) about how amazing you are. I know you're not used to it. I know it's not easy. And I know that your upbringing did not teach you to do that, but you must advocate for yourself. Your route to the life you truly want is through understanding and embracing your most outstanding qualities.

It is something to practice. It is best to make your self-worth real to you by habitually speaking on your behalf. You need to commit to supporting your ability and to rise to the occasion. Be bold and brave. Drop your fear of seeming full of yourself. It isn't helpful to be small, especially if you think that small equals safe. Start claiming the truth of who you are. I'm talking about transcending your issues around telling people the unvarnished truth.

Go ahead, brag about your truth. That will allow you to get used to thinking of yourself in new ways. When no one stops your bragging, no one argues with you, and no one gets offended at your bragging about yourself, you will gradually get used to doing it. And even if people did those things, you'll continue. You will defiantly continue. And eventually, you will work your way around to deeply believing it all yourself. Instead of using your skills to manipulate people into thinking you're harmless, or to get people to like you, it's time to use those skills to find peace with your best qualities.

It's imperative that you relax and shift your focus away from whether someone likes you or not. And that you shift your focus onto how to be yourself fully. There is no need to keep trying to survive your childhood. I don't know if your parents are alive. I don't know if they're still in your life—but are their voices alive in your head? There is no need to keep being afraid of them. There's no need to keep using your survival mechanisms to live your days today. Most people you encounter can handle your truth—whatever that truth is. They can tolerate someone who's having a bad day. They can bear someone full of contradictions. They can endure someone who doesn't always know the answer. They can abide someone who isn't being supportive at the moment. People can take you not being what you think they want. And if they can't take it, they don't deserve you in their life.

Habitually Still Wearing the Mask

One last note: We all have times when we fall back into our old patterns. Try not to beat yourself up over those times when the mask-self—the habitual people-pleaser side of you—comes up again. Over time, you will learn not to let a false version of you take over. Do everything you can to stay authentic and not keep score or give a lot of thought to how your personal growth is going. Take things one day at a time, and when old patterns emerge, find some gratitude that you noticed those old habits returning. Then point your mind and your heart to the present moment and move on.

On the School Bus

When I was crafting this book, I made a decisive change in one of my old habits. I completely revolutionized the way I make books. I turned everything on its head. I was searching for a way to connect with you directly. I wanted to connect heart to heart. And yes, I did that a lot in *How to Be You*, but I also wanted to go further. I realized that I thought there was a "right way" to write—a proper way to make a book. So, while writing *How to Be You*, I made a note of stories from my childhood, my adulthood, my time at the monastery, and my relationship. I put them all on cards. And I went through, attempting to pick out the absolute "correct" story for each chapter. It wasn't until recently that I realized there wasn't one "right way" to write and that trying to pick the absolute "best" story wasn't the right method for me. I spent a lot of time, especially in the early writing process, trying to be the right, perfect, most acceptable, most pleasing writer. And I was concerned about what people would think of me! I wanted to write "right."

I realized that the best way for me to do this was by making recordings. I told you a bit about this back in chapter 2. The truth is that I communicate better by speaking. I film videos almost every single day, as a way to talk to my friends and found family on the internet. I wanted this book to grow out of that family feeling and to feel inviting and direct and kind. So I picked up my phone, hit record, and started talking about the most important subjects to me. I had learned at the Buddhist monastery how to channel my inner wisdom and how to take my own advice. And part of that process was to stay in a meditative state. I learned to stay connected to my heart. So that's how these recordings went. I tapped into my heart and shared what was there, and I saw you in my mind's eye the whole time. I chatted with a friend.

And you know what happened? The words and the stories came naturally. Whether a story was the "perfect" story mattered less and less. And whether I was able to say what was in my heart mattered more and more.

I was 100 percent unpopular in school. I was anti-popular. I experienced violence often from the other kids. One day, I had to walk from the back of the class to the front. It was during study hall, and I always sat at the back of the room. My theory was that if the bullies couldn't see me, I'd be out of their bullying minds. But the classroom door was up front, and I needed to use the bathroom. So I walked from the back of the class-room to the front and turned left to walk past the front row of desks to get to the door. There was a bully who always sat in the first row. His position way up front may seem counterintuitive, but this was study hall, and I guess he wanted to be one of the first to leave.

As I passed his desk—one of those (literally old-school!) modular desks with an attached chair—he stuck out his foot. His ankle caught mine, and I tripped. I face-planted right in front of the whole study hall. My heart was racing. I panicked. I was embarrassed. I looked desperately toward the teacher for help. That was always my instinct. I couldn't believe what I saw: The teacher was laughing at me. The bully was laughing above me. I looked at him from my spot on the floor, trying to stand up and fake my dignity. I saw his broad smile and delighted eyes. He spoke. "Watch where you're going, faggot." The teacher laughed even harder.

A few years earlier, when I was in middle school, I was on the bus—I always sat at the *front* of the bus, since the back was reserved for the trendy kids. It was winter, and I often leaned my face against the bus's cold, fogged half window, feeling the glass on my face and watching winter pass by outside, not talking to anyone else. But on this day, I was *summoned* to the back. A kid came up to me and said, "She wants you." He told me to get to the back of the bus. I got nervous. Does a popular kid want to talk to me? Now I was getting even more nervous. I didn't know what was happening. The person who called me to the back of the bus was a high school girl. I honestly didn't know what was going on.

Maybe the cool kids wanted me to be a cool kid? Maybe? Maybe? Part of me was excited that a popular kid in the back of the bus wanted to talk to me. But of course, part of me was also weirded out and anxious. I'd never been back there. I sat in the seat next to her. It was the very, very last seat in what felt like a long, long yellow school bus. I sat down, and she put her hand on my thigh. She said, "I will teach you how to be a real man."

And then she moved her hand . . . somewhere else. I was confused. And sad. I was baffled because my body *reacted*. I didn't know what to make of it all because I knew I had crushes on boys, and I'd never responded to a girl before. I was sad because, even then, although I probably couldn't articulate it, I felt like this was happening because of my queerness. If I weren't so LGBTQ, I thought, I wouldn't be on that black vinyl seat wishing I could fly out through a school bus half window. If it weren't for my queerness, I wouldn't be sitting there feeling the open-window breeze blowing on my face and the high school girl's hand on my body.

The kids on the bus (in the other back seat across the aisle) and the kids in the surrounding seats were laughing. They were pointing and seemed to be having a really good time. That tipped the bus driver off that something was happening. This girl removed her hand, which had been down my jeans. And the bus driver yelled from the front, "Break it up. Move on." I was stunned. I don't know exactly what the bus driver saw or heard, but it seemed important enough for them to tell my parents.

I remember swinging on the swing set in our backyard that day after getting home. I had grown enough that my shoes dragged through the dirt patch worn in the grass beneath the swing. The incident had happened on the way to school. I spent the whole day at school dazed and worried. But at around 3:20 p.m., after my bus got home, I went right to the swing set because it was one of the places where I could feel the freest. I also felt safer because the swing set was up on a bit of a hill; I could see most of the farm. No surprises.

From the swing set, I saw Mom and Dad talking by the house, looking over their shoulders at me, talking, looking, talking, looking, and it seemed very serious. I felt so much shame. I knew precisely why they were talking. I never did speak to them about it, nor them with me. And what I needed was for them to hug me. I was afraid of what other people would think of me. I feared what my parents would think of me. I don't fault them for not mentioning it, though; maybe they didn't know what to do either.

This incident reinforced my idea that I needed to be hyperaware. I knew then, on the swing, that I was all alone. So it was up to me to tighten my inner grip on everything I could control—mostly myself. I needed to be in control of myself so that I could control what other people thought of me, and so that I could be in control of what other people did to me.

Looking back, I'm surprised we never spoke about it. Mom, Dad, and I, or any combination of Mom and I, Dad and I . . . not even a word. And that just reinforced my shame, my hate for myself for the fact that I had "let" something happen to me. The story lives on in my mind as part of my shame foundation. I assumed that my LGBTQ-ness and this series of events were my shame to carry around for the rest of my life. So if you are reading this and you're a parent, please be super kind to your kids. Put this book down. Run to them and tell them that there are no taboo subjects—that they can talk to you about anything they need to. Tell them that you love them, no matter what happens.

And if you are an adult with no kids, please love your inside child. Love the inner child in your backyard on the swing. Please reconnect with the you that you were, watching adults talk *about* you and not *to* you. Tell yourself that you are loved. Tell yourself that there are no off-limits memories. Then you can give up on worrying about what other people think of you. Make how you treat yourself the priority.

And when you have healed your shame—when you have seen and embraced your needs—I know you will care less and less about needing to become the person who gets your needs met by others. So listen, my beautiful reader. I love you. It's okay to put this book down for a few minutes. It's okay to get a snack. It's okay to breathe with the weight of these paragraphs. And please remember, it is heavy, and I lived it.

In Praise of Needy People

A huge part of giving up on people-pleasing (and giving up on being obsessed with what others think of you) is exploring what it means to have needs. It is imperative to be open and honest with yourself about your needs, and it can be a big step to be honest with others about what you need. In short, it's okay to be needy. All of us are. Because of what happened to me, I love reassurance. I love praise and attention and kindness and, yes, I love love. I'm doing it for the attention! I'm needy indeedy! Also, I love that you have needs. I love people with needs. Needs are great. However, if I were going to write a chapter in praise of people with needs, it would have to be a long chapter, because every person who has ever lived and will live, including every person alive now, including you and me, has needs. It may seem obvious, but it still must be said. What I truly want to discuss right now is people who are *up-front* about their needs.

Open people, people who *need* with wild abandon—I love those people! When you were a kid, you thought you were a horrible needy thing. At a certain point, you got the idea that having needs made you a burden and an annoyance, or you might have learned that having needs is dangerous, evil, and wrong. Your caregivers didn't like you having needs. Maybe they were annoyed. Perhaps they were a little self-absorbed. Perhaps they were never given the tools to parent you with unconditional love. But it all affected you deeply. You took your parents' actions to mean "I shouldn't have needs."

But you had them anyway. And you had already begun a lifelong process of pretending not to have needs. But guess what having needs means? You're human. You're like every other human. We all have needs. And significantly, we all can help each other with those needs. Having needs can bring us together and help us feel less lonely. Having needs is part of the beauty of being a human being. When you were a kid, adults convinced you to act like you didn't have requirements. It is why so many of us were told, "You're very mature for your age."

You might think that this was a compliment that implied you were a kid who was acting like an adult, but we weren't acting like adults. Adults were training us to act like people without needs so that they wouldn't have to address them. Being a person without needs is impossible. Your parents may have encouraged you to act out an impossibility.

There is absolutely nothing wrong with needs.

We all went on a journey to fulfill an impossibility, and adults convinced us to use all of our time, care, and attention to "erase" our neediness. There is absolutely nothing wrong with needs. And there is absolutely nothing wrong with us for having them. It's probably been so long since you've thought about your needs that an exercise might be in order. I suggest you take out a piece of paper and list the top five needs you have right now. List what you require right now for love and support. Go ahead, do it.

Okay. You didn't do it. I know you so well because I'm just like you! Don't think I wouldn't know! Now, let's talk about *why* you didn't do it. Did it bring up just a little (or perhaps a lot of) fear in you? Did it feel like you might be exposed if you listed out something you need? All of this is a massive clue to how your mind judges your needs. You may even have voices in your head warning you about needing too much from others.

People who are up-front about their needs are courageous to live in a world where people are not supposed to
have requirements. To be taught that needs are dangerous, to be told that having needs makes you a burden on
other people, and then to state what those needs are anyway? That, to me, is a hero! That, to me, is a brave person.

So if we go back to our exercise for just one moment,
I'm guessing you had a problem figuring out where to
start. We are so removed from what we need that it will
take a while to get back into the childhood swing of asking for it. Babies can't articulate their needs, but they're
certainly not hiding that they need things. Being in emotional states, crying out when you need something, is
something primal in you. What you have a chance to do
now is begin to be in touch with that part of you again.
You can be in touch with your emotional necessities to
such an extent that you can fulfill some of them yourself!
And you can even articulate to someone what your needs
are and how they can help you meet them.

Let's Stop and Think for a Moment

Now give yourself a chance to do the exercise.
Truly consider your needs. You don't need to write
them down unless you'd like to. But be open and
bold with yourself. It does not matter what you
need or whether you can articulate it well. It is
simply essential to practice checking in with what
your needs are.

Once you begin to voice your needs to others, you will learn who respects your needs. You can use this as a barometer to decide who you'd like to have in your life. But if you're running around pretending you don't have needs, you are going to surround yourself with people who are either (1) attracted to the fact that you don't have needs or (2) attracted to the fact that you keep pretending you don't have needs. Or they might be attracted to the false, "likable," need-less you. And one day, they will find out that you have needs. What will you do then? What happens then? You can prevent whatever happens then by being up-front about your needs now.

So what are some things I would put on my list? (Reminder: I do this work myself, and practicing what I preach is hard work, even for me. I'm about to tell you one of my needs as a way to prove it's possible. Written down! In a book!) I need unconditional acceptance. I don't mean that I need someone who necessarily agrees with me or can see my point of view all the time. I don't need people who even "get me," but I do need people in my life who are willing to accept that sometimes human beings make mistakes. Sometimes human beings are sad or in a bad mood. Occasionally human beings get the wrong ideas. Occasionally human beings need to talk things out.

It's been my great pleasure to realize that as I have become more open and honest about my needs, clear communication has helped me build a chosen family of support. As a result, love has surrounded me with people who can "handle" my needs. Every day, people who love me as a person who is open about my needs enrich my life!

Another thing that might go on the list for me is that I need people who are honest about their own needs to be in my life. I can't run around trying to be psychic. I can't just plug into my childhood patterns of trying to please people, anticipating needs I'm guessing they have. I need to relax and have people communicate and ask directly for what they need. And if they do, I can answer whether I can or can't help. Next, we can work on meeting the need together.

Oh! Another thing I need is rest. Just pure, kind periods of letting go and not having to be on.

As you make your list (because I know you will eventually), I hope you start to love your neediness. **You need to be the star in your own life!** Sometimes you need to be the center of attention, and that's great. That's wonderful! That's human. As you continue to *celebrate* your neediness, as you continue to flaunt it, please be very kind. Be extra kind to yourself and extra kind to anyone else who might have needs, which, of course, is all of us.

Loving Yourself Most of All

The most crucial spiritual decision you will make is to stop trying to please others. The decision to stop trying to control what other people think of you is monumental. If you choose to stop trying to please others, you might start to care about pleasing yourself. When you give up on what others think of you, you can focus on what you feel about yourself.

That decision is the hardest decision you'll make. It feels necessary for me to point out how courageous that decision is. We're talking about putting yourself in the starring role of your life even though your family may have taught you that the only safe place for you is in the wings. Your family made you feel like a secondary character and a "supporter." You might have been taught this for systemic reasons like misogyny, racism, or queer-phobia, or it could have had a lot to do with your family dynamic. Maybe another person in the family constantly needed to be a star. You believed that there is safety in staying small for whatever reason. You realized that your most comfortable, safest, "you-est" role was in support of everyone else.

So now, it's time to start making yourself the star, giving up on even *trying* to get people to like you or even *trying* to please people. And that puts you in the starring role of your own life. I understand you think it's selfish. But there's a huge reason why you do. You've seen very few examples of an unselfish star. You probably haven't seen someone in your own life who doesn't care what other people think, who wasn't also dripping in selfishness and egotism. You haven't seen someone free of caring what others think about them who wasn't all about me, me, me.

The truth of the matter is that you can have a starring role *and* widen the shine of your spot-

You can star in your life and help everyone feel like a star in their own lives.

light to include everyone. You can star in your life and help everyone feel like a star in their own lives. That is the true gift of someone whose self-worth has nothing to do with pleasing others. That person shines brightly with ease and gives each person they encounter a beautiful invitation. You, too, can shine that brightly. You, too, can stop your pattern of trying to be the most presentable, pleasing version of yourself for other people. Yes, it feels like an incredible risk. I called it heroic just a while ago. The real reason it's heroic is that you're forging a new path in your life. No wonder it feels dangerous, and no wonder it feels selfish, but you are indeed brave enough.

It's true that one pitfall to watch out for is swinging your pendulum too far. You don't need to *fight* what other people think of you. You don't need to argue. Fighting what others think of you is a pitfall because that's a waste of energy. By now, it's probably clear to you logically, if not in your own lived experience, that you could be the perfect person and still not please everyone. I tried to satisfy hundreds of thousands of people simultaneously with every post. Do you know how difficult that is on the internet?

Do you know what a miserable failure I was at pleasing the whole internet? If you make a social post and say, "I love oranges over mangoes," people will be outraged in your comments that you didn't mention apples. With how our lives and social interactions are structured, you will likely encounter many, many, many people who cling tightly to their opinions and have snap views about you.

Doing It for the Attention . . . and Loving It

As a nonbinary person, I tend to put people on edge. I will walk into the supermarket wearing a dress, and people will have a visceral and adverse reaction. It seems to be deep and almost automatic. And for years, I took that personally. I tried to dress and act "appropriately." I tried to be a certain way and say certain things so that I wouldn't upset people. It was like being a kid all over again. "You can't worry Mom and Dad." As a nonbinary person, I'm basically designed to upset people in this society. It is nearly a certainty. Eventually, I had to accept that this isn't my problem or my fault. I spent years fighting peoples' reactions. It would go like this: Someone—anyone—would stare at me for a very long time with a negative look on their face. At first, I would think it was my fault. *I am awful. If only I didn't stick out. I deserve people judging me. I deserve people's negative reactions because I'm queer and gross.* And then I realized, *Well, that's not true at all. That's not fair to me. There's nothing wrong with being LGBTQ. There's nothing wrong with me.* But I didn't start there. I wanted to prove to everyone that their opinion of me didn't matter—which is a lot like caring what other people think!

I began to fight the judgmental people I met. I would get in their faces and say, "I'll show you. I'll show you who's amazing. It's me! Look at me! I'm amazing!" I would scream at the top of my lungs. But I've chilled out since then. And I've come to a place where I've more deeply embraced the power in who I am and what I represent. I still love attention, but I also love that I have the power to disrupt. I am the walking disruption of everyday thinking. When I don't take that personally, I'm free. I don't have to take any of it on, and I don't have to make anyone else's opinions mine. I don't have to please others or soothe them. And they don't have to like me.

> I wanted to prove to everyone that their opinion of me didn't matter—which is a lot like caring what other people think!

The only thing I have found that truly enriches my life is giving to others without needing to please them. When I give a speech or post a video or go on television, and I say kind things to myself before and after, if I know I will be with myself before and after, I know I am onto something. I've got my own back.

Let's Stop and Think for a Moment

Is there anything you do for the attention? Can you own or even celebrate that behavior? Can you remove the guilt or bad feelings around wanting and needing attention, respect, kindness?

KEY TAKEAWAYS

1. Learn to identify the behaviors you adopted to survive. Drop any habit that is no longer supporting your self-compassion.

2. Start showing the kindness that you give so freely and in abundance to others to yourself.

3. It takes courage to be needy. Build up that courage and, when it is safe, confide your needs in your friends and family, and also don't forget to tell yourself!

4. When you give up on what others think of you, you have the freedom and space to focus on what you feel about yourself.

Chapter 6

Stop Trying to Avoid Anger and Start Standing Up to Abuse

Mom's Anger

When I decided to go no-contact with my mother, I felt very unsure. No surprise there, but I thought it would be helpful to share that I certainly felt wobbly. It wasn't that I was uncertain whether I should do it. I was sure that our relationship was mentally and emotionally toxic for me. What I was unsure about was whether I'd be able to do it. A few months before, I'd realized just how much abuse my childhood contained and that our adult relationship might not be compatible with my healing. It's interesting because I had always known that my father was abusive. He was vicious in outward and visible ways. He tried to use physical violence, his absence, and distance to get me not to be so . . . me—you know, so LGBTQ. And, to his credit, he was able to (kind of) apologize when I was grown, and he was able to articulate *why* many of his actions were problematic and unfair. But Mom was abusive in a more covert way. Although she supported some of my sparkly kid behaviors, she ultimately also wanted me not to be LGBTQ. She tried many methods to get me to be different from who I was, but she did it in a less visible way. It took me a while to realize the wrongness of it, but when I was a kid, my mom wanted or needed me to be a kind of emotional support to her. And that wasn't fair to me. She had unresolved stuff from her childhood, as we all do, but it remained unresolved. And I was encouraged to become the cheerleader, the support system, and her source of kindness.

One of the hardest things for me to comprehend during my time at the monastery was not taking other people's emotions personally. I had become obsessed with "helping" people feel better. I realized after a while that, looking back, I was constantly on edge as a kid because I never knew which mom I would get. When she showed up to pick me up from school, which mom would be behind the wheel? Would she be the kind, caring mom who so lovingly microwaved the SpaghettiOs when I felt sick? Would she be the angry, frustrated mom who lashed out with false accusations, asking a small kid, "How could you do this to me?" I remember thinking, *Do what? I don't even know what I did.* I did know exactly how to tell which mother was in front of me. I was a young child, but I had a detailed mental list of every sigh and gesture and vibe of my mother. I was always attempting to read her so that I could spring into action. So that I could cheer her or console her or run away. And if I couldn't console her, I felt like a complete failure. For years, I went around saying "I'm an empath," but I was simply trained to laser-focus on emotional signals from people who weren't happy.

I remember many times when my mother would be angry at my dad and then complain to me as if I were one of her girlfriends. "How could he do this to me again?" she would say, as if a six-year-old knew why adults did anything to each other. Yes, many times, she was delightful, supportive, and she sacrificed a lot. But many times, she was The Mother, angry and on a rampage of frustration and blame. I would get hit. I would get yelled at. I would get punished for things I couldn't know anything about. And sometimes, I would be let into her inner world. It felt like a special place. Being her "little confidant" gave me a place to belong, but I couldn't make that mom stay. I couldn't be the right-enough child to help her feel predicably good. I still viscerally remember the unpredictable and volatile heat of her anger when she was in one of her moods. For years, the chaos felt like my fault. I believed that if I was a perfect child or a better consoler, I could have healed her and brought about a peaceful family.

I wrapped up my worth in how best I could serve and support her, and eventually, she helped me tie my worth to how best I could be of service to other people. I realized all this in the months leading up to no-contact time. And I wondered if I would be able to leave. But one day, I knew in my gut that it was time. I got a text from Mom that said something about coming home, a visit for my father's birthday in July. And I simply texted back, "I'm not going to be in contact with the family for a while." It was messy, and it was imperfect, and it was the best I could do at the time. And she sent back a text in angry all-caps. "WHAT THE F DOES THAT MEAN?" I was unsure if I would be able to follow through on going no-contact because I was still, as an adult over forty years old, suffering from a kind of emotional Stockholm syndrome. I could see, and I could honor, that her parents didn't treat her well. I could also observe that her childhood hadn't prepared her for a healthy relationship with me. She certainly wasn't given the skills to raise a vibrantly LGBTQ child. And I wasn't sure if my natural empathy would cause me to (guiltily) stay in contact. But Mom's response text gave me an epiphany. I saw it all in her ALL-CAPS attempt to guilt me: It was a requirement that I deny my own experience— that I never acknowledge or talk about the damage she had done to me throughout my childhood. To have a relationship with her meant that I must discard or ignore my experience. I must trash, deny, and set aside my experience. For just a moment, a moment of grace, I imagined a different possibility. I imagined another mother, like a shaft of light coming through a church window, who could hold, accept, understand, attempt to discuss, or respect my experience. Another mother who might *want* to change or make peace or talk out or honor why I might make a no-contact decision. The disparity between my mom's text and that image was stark.

The realization that I had denied everything I had been through and everything she had done to blunt my self-esteem and personal happiness for decades made me extremely angry. But once I was able to see that anger as a matter of justice versus injustice, I could also see the humanity of both of us. I could see my humanity and why I do some of the things I do. I could see the profound unfairness of requiring your child never to bring up problematic things that had happened. I could see the injustice of requiring your child to talk about the family in always-rosy terms, an incredibly unfair requirement when our family got quite dark growing up. When I could see that unfairness, I knew that no-contact had been the correct answer. I could see that no-contact was my spiritual way to honor myself instead of honoring the narrative she wanted. So, I gave up on her narratives, and I was finally able to relax. I didn't need to stick around. I didn't feel a need to fight her. I didn't feel a need to stand up for what I had experienced. I didn't feel compelled to right the injustice with her. I could right it on my own. Interestingly, to this day, I don't harbor any ill will at all toward either of my parents. *And,* I will not be contacting them for quite some time, or maybe ever. This is how I have honored myself and how I have used my anger to drop my learned behaviors and start to heal. Going no-contact with my family was a large part of my healing process.

Let's Stop and Think for a Moment

Have you considered ending contact with someone? Consider how often guilt informs that type of decision. If you are considering ending contact with a family member, ask yourself this: What kind of person ends contact with a family member? A bad person? A mean person? Challenge your assumptions about who you are by undoing these labels around going no-contact.

When my first book, *How to Be You*, came out, I remember a phone conversation I had with my mom. It happened a few weeks after the book went on sale, after a launch event I had. Mom and I got on the phone, and I wanted her to say, "You were the first nonbinary person to work with a major publisher. That's amazing. Congratulations on your accomplishment. Thank you for being a trailblazer." I expected her to say, "You've saved many young people's lives. You inspire so many people by being yourself. I'm so happy that you told your story." She didn't say that. She didn't say, "I'm proud of you." She didn't say, "What a great book." Instead, she said, "How could you tell that story about me?" She meant the story of my coming-out. Or, you could say, it is the story of her mishandling my coming-out, which I discussed earlier, but to recap: At eleven years old, we were in the car together, and I stumbled and fumbled into these words: "I think I like boys." And she got pretty angry. She slammed on the brakes and turned the wheel hard in a theatrical fashion. She started yelling, "You don't know anything about that. You're too young. Don't ever talk about that again." I felt . . . um . . . awful. My palms were sweaty, and my heart beating a mile a minute. She raised her voice again, a vein in her neck pulsing. She told me in no uncertain terms that I didn't know what my experience meant. I was too young to understand why sharing myself was such an angering experience for her.

I got the deep-seated message that day that something was wrong with me. And I also got the news that to avoid her total rejection and anger, and to avoid losing her love, I needed to hide the most poetically rainbow, beautiful part of who I am. She would later tell me she yelled because she feared AIDS. She was afraid that I would be a pariah—scared that if I were LGBTQ, I would be diseased and lonely. And all of that makes sense to me. That was what the media and the broader culture had told her being LGBTQ was. But her anger didn't make sense to me. And eventually, her anger made *me* angry. As I worked through and navigated the fact that she made the launch of my first book about the stories I had told *of her*, it finally began to sink in that the true injustice was the imbalance of power between us. No matter how old I got, I couldn't be her equal. Her need to set the narrative was not compatible with my spiritual health and growth. We're still no-contact today as I write this. And my anger over her anger has subsided. I now feel that the best way to right this injustice is to continue to have no-contact. No talking, no fighting, and no "teaching her a lesson." So today, I've decided that we'll be growing and living in separate places, with independent lives. Sometimes it is best to live going in separate directions.

Anger and Injustice

The best thing that anger can do is point you toward justice, in your relationship with your family and with your world. Anger is an *essential* emotion, but many people spend their whole lives running from it, trying to avoid it, having problems with it, trying to conquer it, trying to get over it, and never precisely seeing it for what it is. At its best, anger is a call to fairness and a hand stretched out in your direction—an invitation to honor how much you care.

I came home one day, my feet in six-inch heels and aching from the walk back from the subway. This was about two years ago, and Jeff's shoes were in a spot where my shoes go. I was standing in the entryway of our tiny New York City apartment, and we had three locations for shoes by the door. We sensibly agreed to use those spots for our most frequently worn shoes. And Jeff is a bit more of a fashionista than I am (but only a bit!). Believe it or not, he has more shoes than I do. And usually, he kept his two most-worn pairs of shoes in spots two and three, and my shoes would go in spot one. I came home on this day, and Jeff's shoes occupied spots two and three. And also spot one. He had worn special-occasion shoes. He took them off by the door. He put his shoes in *my* spot. I glared at his shoes. My blood began to boil. I felt fiery, intense, white-hot anger at his thoughtless, self-absorbed shoe flinging. Anger flooded my whole system. I started shaking. I was so angry, and yet in that moment, I could also see that the anger was outsized—it was way too big for the circumstance—it was inappropriate.

So I began to breathe. Years of meditation were paying off! I began to look very carefully at the anger and those shoes, not in a judgy way, like, "It's just shoes. Why are you getting so upset?" I wouldn't allow self-hate—no self-judgment for being angry, just feeling and looking. I sidestepped any programming or voices that my parents instilled in me, and I breathed and looked. One unusual thing that happened that day was that I welcomed the anger. You could say I *respected* it. It came to visit, and I said yes, and I watched it. And what I realized eventually is that the trigger for that anger was Jeff's shoes in spot three, Jeff's shoes in spot two, and Jeff's shoes in spot one. It was a matter of *unfairness*. I could see that all the spots were filled, including what I knew was my spot. I watched a story in my mind: "It was already unfair that he had two spots and you only get one. And to add to that, now he has three spots, and you have zero." That's a tragedy, that's a travesty, that's unfairness. And so I breathed with that unfairness. That day, I could feel the anger reaching back through time to my childhood. It grasped every injustice from my time as a kid and dragged it all forward into the present with long fingers. The intensity of the shoe-place anger was the intensity of an anger for my whole life, an emotional synecdoche for all the anger I had stuffed down. Every time I was bullied or told I was going to hell or got hit . . .

This tiny moment triggered a wave of anger for *every* time people had wronged me. As a kid, I seldom got to right the wrongs done to me. And the huge intense wrongs that people had done to me as a child were now flung out by my anger on my beautiful partner's three pairs of shoes like past-trauma vomit, pooling by the door in our apartment. And I could see it. I could see Little Jeffrey being subjected to all that injustice. I could see why "simple things" like shoes made me so full of rage. I'm very grateful for spiritual practice, because I could have yelled at Jeff without a breath, without looking. I could have withheld affection from Jeff. I could have ranted and raved and been angry for days at Jeff. I could have employed all the anger techniques I saw as a kid. Then, in a flash of inspiration, and of self-kindness, I made space to invite the anger in, and the rage became okay. I was free, and I could see how far back the bitterness and vitriol went. Shoes of today walking back to a five-year-old me, and taller and more significant people being mean and abusive. And for years, I had to stuff my anger down. I had to hide it and just deal with it. And I felt so powerless as a young person. There was just no way to do anything about the injustice in my life.

Let's Stop and Think for a Moment

What triggers your anger? Think back to how your anger was handled when you were growing up. Was anger an acceptable emotion or unacceptable? Was anger okay for someone else in your home, but not for you? What makes you angry today? Are unfairness and injustice triggers for you? Do self-absorbed people trigger you? Did you grow up around anyone who was self-absorbed?

Of course, I'm marginalized as a nonbinary person, and there is still injustice in my life and the world. And what's intriguing is that clueless, self-absorbed people, who act in selfish ways, are the most significant source of my anger today. And now I've made the connection. That anger primarily comes from the self-absorbed adults who were in my life in my childhood. They didn't notice me, and they rarely cared. Self-absorption is a trigger for me because I have unhealed injustice in my childhood. Almost no one ever asked, "How are you doing?" I remember feeling so powerless. I couldn't get anyone's attention. And the thing I do have power over now, the thing I can do immediately (and you can do it too) is practice recognizing that anger points to injustice. Today, I can do the work of healing. I can work to heal the injustice within. We can all take a vow not to treat ourselves the way adults treated us when we were kids. That's what I went away to the monastery to learn. I had taken on the abandonment and the nitpicking of my childhood. I was doing that inside. I was treated terribly as a kid, and I had taken on the role of my parents within myself. The self-beatings, the self-violence, what you could call the self-anger. "How could you do such a thing? How could you?" I became an A+ student of a now-internal language of violence and anger. "They're going to laugh at you. You deserve this. How could you?"

> **We can all take a vow not to treat ourselves the way adults treated us when we were kids.**

Those internal beatings are maybe the ultimate form of injustice. And that's why I value my spiritual practice.

My anger is connected to injustice. Your childhood experiences may have caused you to stifle outrage and try to keep it at bay. And we are taught, through experience, that anger is a form of abuse. It's possible that the only anger we ever saw as kids was concurrent with abusive behavior. So, when we experience anger today, we might think we are exactly like our abusers. I don't know about you, but in the household I grew up in, violence was coming if either of my parents were angry. I learned that anger puts me in incredible danger. The one thing that is clear about traumatized people is we know what it feels like for someone to abuse us. And most of us never want to do that to someone else. It can create some of the most severe self-hate if our childhood trauma patterns hurt someone else.

So in my story about the shoes, I could have yelled at Jeff in a moment of deep anger. I could have yelled at Jeff and gotten as angry with him as my parents often got with me. The guilt and the bad feelings would've followed, and it would have been intense. And maybe that has happened to you. Perhaps your childhood trauma has snuck out through anger—through a pressure building within you toward violence. And if that anger or violence was released onto other people, you might have noticed that feeling bad and guilty afterward does not prevent it from happening again.

But I'm going to tell you what does help prevent it, or at least what has worked for me: Concentrate on justice and making the world fair. Concentrate on helping others and yourself to have an equitable life. Make your anger righteous by devoting yourself to the ultimate equity: an end to violence in the world. And while you're at it, commit to stopping the violence you're committing within yourself. As I allow anger in, I find that there can be peace surrounding it. If I can focus on serenity within when I am angry, that helps me to transmute the anger into a drive for justice. I make my life about peace within myself and in the world. And that process of living in harmony, being committed to peace, adoring peace, and celebrating peace, even when I am

Commit to stopping the violence you're committing within yourself.

angry, truly helps me heal. As ironic as it sounds, I have cultivated a peaceful relationship with anger. I think of anger as a visitor, as someone who comes to remind me of the importance of justice.

One of the keys to spiritual practice is divorcing a behavior from an emotion. Almost every emotion has an attached behavior. Emotions make the stories in our heads seem real. And once specific stories seem real, certain behaviors feel inevitable. It's possible that when you were a kid, big feelings often accompanied significant danger—at least, that's how it was for me. So, today, when you feel a big emotion like anxiety or anger, you believe a whole host of narratives about the situation and the other person, and you want to *do something*. To me, my personal assumptions about why Jeff placed the shoes there and what he thought of me all seemed very real. "That's my spot. How dare Jeff take my spot?" I thought I needed my spot and should do what I needed to do to get it. I had never before realized that, when I was angry, I was not trying to right a wrong that was happening in the moment but a wrong that had happened to me between ages zero and eighteen. The reason it's important to notice what you think is supposed to happen next, be it yelling at your partner or with-holding affection, is because that sequence of events is a story you have internalized. And that way could easily hurt you and others. Habitual actions like that can't heal. What happened to you when you were a kid? You have to remedy that directly. You can't cure it by proxy.

If I hadn't been able to divorce the emotion from the behavior, I wouldn't have been able to breathe and witness and watch and heal that day. I would've been too busy yelling. But what I was able to do was have enough space to see a very young Jeffrey who was alone, who had no one to help save them. I remembered a very young Jeffrey who had no advocates. And that is at least partly where the fierceness, the enthusiasm, and the energy of the anger originates.

When I was at the monastery, we talked about anger being a finger pointing at the moon. Anger is the finger, and the moon is what they would call a "secondary emotion" related to anger. The classic secondary emotion is a sense of sadness or a sense of not belonging—a sense of separation. The moon in that image is big, broad, celestial, massive, and poetic. The finger is tiny. But we look at the finger, concentrating on the anger. We're even *encouraged* by our family and the adults around us growing up to focus on the finger-anger, and hate ourselves for being angry. Many of us learn to be afraid that our anger makes us just like our father or mother. But of course, if we can learn to look where the finger is pointing—if we can see what our mother and father never got to know about themselves—we will see that our anger is trying to right a long-past wrong. And when we see it, we have a chance for healing. If we can see the big picture, we have an opportunity to change our lives completely.

The other element to address regarding anger is activism. You can use your anger to activate yourself and stand up to real abusers. Standing up to people acting unjustly, who fuel injustice in the world, will close the loop for you and help heal the moments from your past when you couldn't stand up for justice. This "pure anger" or "aware anger" can be part of your activism. It can be energy directed toward creating justice.

Standing up to abusers can be commonly referred to as "setting boundaries." But honestly, I think that phrase is a bit overused. I would instead think of it as clear communication. Clear communication can look like no-contact from here on out. Or it can be saying, "This is what our limited contact will look like," or it can be any number of things. Standing up to abusive people in our day-to-day lives includes fully allowing and experiencing your anger while also looking past it toward the moon. If you're aware of the moon—the primary emotion hiding beyond your anger—the anger can't force you to act in any particular way. Abusive people can't force you to do what *they* want. Often, mean people will use our anger to turn the tables and try to make us think we are the problem. But we are not the problem. If we can be at peace with having anger, manipulative people can't force us to believe their narrative. They can't press our buttons, can't trigger us to do their bidding, because we're aware that, deep down, we might be motivated by a sense of not belonging. Ironically, we might be driven to anger by our sense of compassion for people being mistreated or by our compassion for our own sensitivity. If you feel anger at a very intense level, if it comes on quickly, if it feels mysterious and sudden, and if it seems out of proportion to the original event, this is a place to look: You care about justice. You care about equity for your six-year-old self. You care deeply. And when things are unjust, you get angry. And yes, the fact that you care doesn't mean you are automatically a pushover for abusive people. As you embrace your anger, you'll notice that abusive people in your life are also a matter of justice.

You don't deserve any abuse, and it shouldn't continue. Abusers shouldn't continue to abuse you, even if you have felt loyal to them for your whole life. You need to stand up if you have the strength for it. It doesn't have to be perfect, and it will take some practice, but standing up to abuse and fighting the injustices in the world (and in your family or church or school) will undoubtedly help you heal. Anger is a friend who can help you heal. I think this is what people mean when they talk about anger as *righteous*. If anger is fuel in the fight for equality, it is also fuel in the battle for healing.

Anger is a friend who can help you heal.

The Parts of Anger

Earlier, we looked at how anger is built upon a story. Anger is a narrative—language in your mind feeds and stokes anger: "How dare they. People shouldn't act that way." And on and on. But you may not have realized that the parts of anger can be dissected. We can look frankly at what makes up your anger, and we can work toward unraveling all that goes with anger. Anger is, after all, energy in the body. So let's break down anger into its constituent parts. Anger contains three different components that all get lumped together into its emotional label. First, there is a *sensation* in the body, a literal feeling within your body. When I feel anger, it's a fiery sensation near my sternum. It's like a burning electric feeling that propels me to action. That set of body sensations is labeled as anger, and that label is also a *story*. The story is the second part of the emotion, the part that builds on the way anger makes you feel physically, and this word, *anger*, becomes a conversation in your head: "She hates me. This isn't fair. Why is she judging me? I don't deserve this. Who does she think she is? How dare she do this to me? I can't believe she said that." You talk to yourself about who you are and who others are and why they do what they do and who is right and who is wrong—telling yourself the story behind your anger. And then finally—the third piece, the piece that most people don't understand—is that all of this blossoms into a *behavior*. So, "How could she say that" is linked to treating her (whoever "her" is) awfully, or teaching her a lesson, or being mean, or being aggressive, or even being physically violent, or allowing vengeance or hate to guide you. Whatever it is, there's a behavior fastened to the emotion, triggered by the feelings in your body.

So let's break it down. With anger, we have sensations in the body. We have a word and a narrative story, and then we have a behavior. Our reactions to anger— the story and the behavior associated with it—don't allow us any space to choose a different course of action. But, if you start to look at your anger and identify those three different stages, anger will become less overwhelming. It may even become so familiar that it loses some of its power.

If you try to look at that story directly, you'll notice that it's very hard to see it. The story is generally so subtle and so background and behind the scenes that it's seldom evident that it's linked to your long-ago past. Almost all children are treated unfairly from time to time. There are moments when our needs and our fair treatment are steamrolled under our parents' wishes or ignored when a sibling receives more attention and better support than us. We can receive the message "you don't deserve the same treatment as others" in a million ways as children, even with the most loving and delightful parents. If the unfairness of your young life had a profound effect on you, you may have become obsessed with justice and fairness and making things equal. And anger follows a deeply seated pattern within you, like wagon wheels on a well-worn dirt road. The pattern won't change unless you change it. It's a story built on what happened to you in the past. So, as you begin to heal from past trauma, you will naturally start to heal your anger. But again, I want to emphasize there's no need to cure today's anger. So many people who come to me for one-on-one coaching wish to get rid of their anger. And I say, no, please don't even try to get rid of it. You could say anger is a gift. Anger is a visitor. And I would go further than that. Anger is a tool.

Anger is your alarm system.

Anger is your alarm system. Anger reminds you to focus inward and take care of yourself—or it *can* remind you of that. And all of the parts of anger (when we disconnect it from any behavior) are acceptable. Feelings in your body and a story in your head aren't necessarily dangerous.

Let's Stop and Think for a Moment

What makes you angry? Who makes you angry? Recall a recent time when you were totally steamed. If that anger was a gift, if the anger was trying to tell you something, what would it say? Would the situation have been different if you'd assumed the anger was fighting for you? What if the anger was a reminder that you deserve respect?

The part of the equation that usually gets our attention is the behavior. The feelings and the story cause us to do something we "must" do, and it usually isn't pretty. It's usually "not like us."

So, the part of the anger that might get us in trouble is the behavior. I know this sounds completely radical: You can be completely and justifiably angry and not do anything about it. It isn't what your parents taught you, and it sounds off the wall. It might sound like I'm speaking a different language, but try this: Feel the sensations. Recognize what you're feeling. You can even begin to listen to your internal dialogue about how your anger is justified without getting caught up in that story, and you can *not act*. You can *not behave in the way the head-story wants you to behave*.

You can be completely and justifiably angry and not do anything about it.

With time and practice, you can broaden your choices. You can choose a different behavior.

We must bolster all spiritual awakenings with a behavior change. There is no change in consciousness without a behavior change. They work together. And we tend to assume that a new behavior must always come *after* a realization—that when we *know* better, we will do better. But sometimes you can change a behavior at the same time as your understanding changes. You could even experiment with changing a behavior that causes you suffering "just because" and then work your way into a new understanding of the situation. For sure, being able to divorce any usual behavior from a story in your head will help you grow and realize new things about life and yourself.

And that's why I told the story about my mom's reaction to my first book. My well-worn-anger story would have had me yelling at her, raving, raging, and *making sure she understood what she had done to me.* And since I was able to separate that behavior from the story in my head—since I could see that I have choices—I was free. Instead of "having" to do any of those things, I went no-contact. I cut contact with her without yelling or lesson teaching. I had tried an angry approach before (many frustrating times), allowing my anger to lead us through a discussion of my childhood and her hand in it. I often imagined I could "teach her a lesson." But that does not work. Instead, I made a healthy choice for my emotional and mental health. And I didn't do the everyday, obvious behavior pattern that goes with the narrative. I didn't choose the behavior that goes with the label and the sensations of anger.

If you'd asked me about all of this ten years ago, I would have told you that I did not get angry. That I wasn't that kind of person. But the truth is that I completely bottled up my anger. As a kid, I had space to be sad, because I could do that in my room alone. I suppose I could have also been angry in my room alone, but anger was a more outward emotion, and I remember it was forbidden. I couldn't show the power of anger. Being angry meant standing up for myself or something I believed in, and I couldn't do that with my parents. It would never have flown. I may have tried once and gotten so "disciplined" by them that I never would've gone there again. But being sad was safe.

And so I spent years and years being sad. And I spent years and years assuming I'm not an angry person. But guess what? I am. I am furious sometimes. The thing that convinced me and broke the outrage dam was hitting a pillow. Years ago, one of my friends convinced me to get angry. My ex, B., had just broken up with me. My first long-term relationship was over, by his choice. And he decided that, since we lived in New York City, we had to continue our living situation. Oh, and also he was selfish and a jerk. That was hard. But he also decided he would become a porn actor while we were still living together. I loved him, and he was very publicly with other people, and we were still physically connected, as roommates.

It was heartbreaking and devastating, but I didn't get angry. I was despondent, but because of my childhood programming, I didn't realize that I was also immensely angered by his actions, deep down. And I honestly had no idea until my friend sent me into her bedroom. She said, "I'm going to set a timer. You can't come out of my bedroom until you hit the pillow on the bed several times, as hard as you can." We had been talking about this ex and his choices. She could tell that

I was angry, and I assume she could tell that I was denying it, suppressing it, and pushing it down. And she thought, *Well, let's help Jeffrey bring it out.* That day changed my life. I'll never forget it for as long as I live because the longer I hit the pillow, the more I realized that the anger was okay. The energy itself was okay. It wasn't hurting anybody.

I grew up around an angry father and an angry mother, and whenever anger was present, violence or abuse would almost always follow. So, I began to associate anger with abuse. And I didn't realize it was even possible to be angry *and* non-abusive. I didn't realize it was possible to be angry *and* nonviolent. And so I lived "without anger." I spent years thinking, *I'm not a person who gets angry.* I also thought that because I'm not a violent person, anger is not an issue for me. I never realized this until the rage flowed out of my heart through my arms and into my friend's bedding. I allowed the emotion to explode out of my childhood and into the present moment of pummeling pillows. Those poor pillows! The white-hot rage streamed out of me. And the massive enlightening realization that the energy of anger could flow and pour out, tumble out and rumble out, without hurting me or anyone else, was striking. It was a final, final realization (and an absolutely enlightening experience) that I'm worth something, that there are parts of me that this ex had hurt, and that my dad had hurt. And all parts of me, especially the young-feeling parts, are worth defending.

KEY TAKEAWAYS

1. The unfairness and wrongdoings we have experienced follow us. And that is okay. Every life is a mosaic of pain and triumph and difficulty and joy. You can embrace it all.

2. Emotions develop associated behaviors over time, and we must work to make those behaviors kind to us.

3. Going no-contact with abusers is more effective than setting boundaries. Recognizing the power that your presence has in their life—and taking that away—can have a massive impact.

4. Identify and familiarize yourself with the contours of your anger. Embrace your anger, but don't let it control you. Anger can be the first sign that you are taking your own needs seriously.

Dear Little Jeffrey, Age Thirteen

Oh, you are so cute! I love it. And you are so talented. Ahh, I know you have crushes, and I want to talk to you about that. But first, I have to compliment you. You sing so beautifully! You perform and bring the house down with comedy, make people cry, and let people know they're not alone. Your talent is so beautiful. And I'm irate that you keep getting cast as inanimate objects and older adults in every school play. It's not fun to be the tree! It's frustrating that you get cast as those things at the community theater as well.

But this is unfortunately the story of our life. People will have a hard time putting us in any category, and now that you're a teenager, I know you resent that deeply. Later, with you on my mind, I start to enjoy being uncategorizable. I'll begin to enjoy my need for attention and not being easy to place! But you don't have to worry about any of that now. We break molds, and we love attention, and sadly, we're going to get cast as the outsider and the background "odd storyteller" for years to come. LGBTQ folks, nonbinary kids, especially during your "now," in the 1980s, are outside the system. There aren't any plays about us. There are no musicals about our experience. And there is no way that the community theater or your school would let you play Reno Sweeney like you want. That stinks. I love you deeply. And even though nobody can see who you are, and nobody can see your genuine need to be the star you are, I can see it. And I find you beautiful. Maybe people can see who you are, and they're just afraid. But that's not your problem; that's a discussion for another day.

I love that you're still playing dress-up, even though thirteen is past the age when you're "supposed to." Please keep expressing yourself! The barn is still where you belong. You've created such a loving space for yourself in secret. I love that you're still sneaking off to pretend to be Julie Andrews. Of course it's behind closed doors, and I know it still makes you nervous that you might get caught. But you are making beauty out of muck, exquisite places out of being outcast, and beautiful musicals out of cold silence. You're creating full-on elaborate stage productions with your whole heart. It's beautiful! I'm so happy that you still sing for the cows and perform for the slatted barn walls. I love you very much, Jeffrey.

It's frustrating that you can't tell anyone about Michael S. and your crush on him. Your need to express and show love is touching. When you're thirteen and like us, it's terrifying to consider what other people will think of you having crushes on boys. But (in case it helps) let me tell you what I think of you. You are amazing. You are a beautiful teenage soul. You have created a life for yourself where you get a chance to shine and thrive under some of the most stressful circumstances. You can exude star power as a toy boat in The Velveteen Rabbit unlike anybody else I've ever seen. You can charm people. You can show them a side of themselves that they've never known. We can't control what other people think of us, and we will never be able to, but I love you across all time and our timeline.

You are important! Your crushes are essential! The way you feel about Michael (and some of the other boys in your class) is one of the most beautiful things about you. Joy is always beautiful. You genuinely feel ready to sacrifice, support, and give with your heart to another human being. It's lovely, and yes, you deserve the chance to talk to other people your age, or other people in general, about how cute and crushable some of those boys are in your class. But I'm angry that you will never get the chance. I'm angry that the bullies make fun of you—even adult bullies. I'm angry that you are afraid of the big loud yellow school bus.

It's unfair that you have a lot of acne and that the kids at school make fun of how femme you are and how you look. My heart is with you. I know you've started to make elaborate plans to avoid the bullies. I know you've worked out how to walk home from school by hiding in the bathroom after the bell rings until a specific time. I know you've worked out where to sit "inconspicuously" on the bus and what route to take out of the school building to avoid the bullying and beatings. I know you've done a lot of planning to prevent physical violence every day. But—I know that you face violence when you get home too. And I know that you've made plans to avoid that violence. You've schemed to be safe and to survive. Thank you.

Also, I know that all this violence makes you angry. I

know that anger makes you afraid. Afraid and angry. An-
gry and afraid. I know you would do anything you could
to avoid that anger. It reminds you of Dad so much. I
understand that the violence also makes you sad (like it
would make anyone miserable). I know how unfair it
all feels and how horrible it is that no one is helping
you. I want to tell you that your anger and your sadness
are okay. I want to tell you that we're forty-four now, and
I've devoted my whole life to stopping abuse because of
you. I always try to help kids like you. I've done it all be-
cause of you. And by the way, I wasn't able to be free
enough to stand up to abusers until I genuinely felt and
honored your anger.

You care so much what the kids at school think of you.
Of course you do! To get through each day, you've tried
to make everybody believe that you are straight and cis-
gender. I know that you quote the Bible a lot still and you
pretend to have crushes on girls. You asked Becky to see
Godspell *at the dinner theater. I know it makes you angry*
that Becky took you out to the parking lot, during Jesus's
musical crucifixion, to make out. I know that you didn't
want to go and kiss her by the dumpsters. I know that it
all felt profoundly uncomfortable and invasive when she
stuck her tongue into your mouth. I also know that Becky
grossed you out. She had blueberry pie stuck in her brac-
es. If it helps you feel less alone, I can't eat blueberry pie
to this day. It's too awful, and it is connected to too many
bad memories.

I think of you often and how you make all these intel-

ligent, elaborate plans. Safety plans. Procedures for (conditional, but all you know is possible right now) acceptance. I think about how you've devoted your brain and your whole self to a life of planning for and around cis and straight people. I know that the planning was programmed into you for years . . . scheming to control what they think of you and how they treat you for years! And I don't know if you've realized yet the incredible intelligence it has taken for you to plan around avoiding (trying to avoid!) the reactions of other people. It's brilliant to lay these multistep plans for survival. It is genius to apply these plans so that other people will not suspect or think you are LGBTQ. You have a girlfriend! You love blueberry pie! You plan so that you will survive. You plan so that you will avoid their violence, their mean looks, and their ridicule. So, much of your life is devoted to preventing Mom's rage and contact with Dad's fists. You live in an outraged, violent, and chaotic world, and I wish I could make you safe.

I want you to know that you are safe with me. If you ever want to come to visit me and say hello here in our secure future, you don't have to plan ten steps ahead around me. You can simply be yourself. I would love to talk to you about plays, singing, dancing, crushes, how you can't wait to drive, dresses, nail polish, and everything you don't get to talk about at home. I would love to talk about all the beautiful things that make you, you. I know you've seen David Bowie, and I know you've seen RuPaul, and I know you found that dusty library copy of Christine Jorgensen's biog-

raphy. I understand that all these ideas about how to express yourself and what you might be when you grow up are swimming through your head. And I know that the possibility of it all is simply delicious. And I also know that you're terrified that someone will find out that you love those possibilities. I know you feel like Jesus doesn't love you. I know you feel like the possibilities of your whole gendered self are your shame. I know you try to control what other people think of you by hiding the flowering of your soul.

I know you have a habit now, to survive, of being small. I know you have no one to sit with you at lunch. You can sit with me anytime you want. I remember your least favorite moment, holding your tray at the end of the lunchroom line, panic setting in. Where should I sit? You've gotten into the habit of going way off to the side of the lunchroom to sit by yourself—quickly!—because that's better than looking around in panic, begging people with your eyes to let them sit with you. I also know that sometimes you avoid the lunchroom altogether and hide out in the library during lunch because books have never judged you. I wish I could be there with you. And maybe by some miracle, you feel me cheering you on and sitting down to eat with you.

I also know that your body is changing in ways that you hate . . . Your body is growing more hair, and altogether, you're losing the softer, more feminine aspects of who you are that you have always loved. I feel for you so deeply.

You are a shining light to the world. You are a bright, beautiful spot in a school, in a church, and a world in which many people are committed to darkness. I know it scared you when the KKK marched down the main street by your church. I know you felt like you couldn't talk to anyone about your fear of hate. I know you made a pact with yourself to hate yourself more than anyone else could so that you could feel some control in an out-of-control life. And I know it scares you to think of your future and wait many more years before you can leave the farm and the hate and the small-mindedness and indeed be yourself. I know you aren't sure and that you hope college will be a joyful place—an accepting place where you can be out and open. My heart is with you while you wait. I will build a place where you belong. I will make a family for us, and I will build it because of you. I will help us both move past what other people think of us to concentrate on how much we love each other. And yes, as an adult, as a forty-four-year-old human, I will celebrate and honor your anger at how unfair the world can be. I will use your anger as the starting point to stand up to bullies. Thank you for who you are.

Write a letter to yourself at age thirteen. What were you into then? Did you have a special hobby or interest you haven't thought about in years? What did that habit say about who you were as a person? Did you "know what you want(ed) to be when you grew up"? Give yourself some sound advice and encouragement. Thank your young self for being authentically you.

Part 3

Embody the Spiritual Principles of Fearlessness

Once you have strengthened your relationship with yourself and changed your dynamic with others, you are free to become fearless. I mean that word quite literally. Once you prove to yourself that you have your own back—that you can be with yourself in kindness no matter what happens—you will live without fear. If you know that you can be gentle and loving with yourself before, during, and after any stressful moment in your life, you don't need to fight with life so hard. You don't need to control, cajole, or push so hard to have the life you think you should. Once you practice self-kindness often enough that it becomes a new habit for you, you can relax.

You can relax because you don't need to keep your life "together." You don't need to meet a single standard. You don't have to seem like you're put together. You don't need to impress, convince, or spend any time showing people that you are anything other than what you naturally are. That is a truly fearless person. You can begin accepting your place in the flow of life and admit that you know a thing or two. You can give up on being someone else's idea of together and allow the wisdom of your heart to guide you. You can give yourself the very best advice.

And part of that journey will be accepting that your life, like everyone's life, has been filled with pain from time to time. Instead of running from your pain, you can feel it. If you know deep down that you will accept yourself no matter what happens, you can finally be okay with how difficult and painful and unfair life can be. You may even begin to celebrate that you are a sensitive and feeling person. I would rather feel the problematic pain of life than spend another minute trying to cut off all my feelings. In a way, I am proud of my pain and am pleased that I love all of myself and my past, even the parts that are painful to remember. All of it has made me, me. And I love all of it. I want to teach you to love all of you too.

Chapter 7

Stop Trying to Get Your Life Together and Start Enjoying Unpredictability

walk a lot in my beautiful Los Angeles neighborhood. We have many sunny days here. So, walking has lately become my favorite form of exercise. I was walking just last week, and someone had used what I might call good old-fashioned fertilizer on their front lawn. I recognized the smell right away. We do love green and natural things here in Los Angeles! The smell brought me back to the farm. I was struck by memory and stuck on the sidewalk. My feet paused automatically. Without my permission, prediction, and ability to prevent it, I was six years old in the sunshine of a lonely summer day in rural Pennsylvania. Most of us, for our whole lives, have been led to believe that we are in control—or that we should be. You need to control your emotions and feelings and thoughts and mind chatter and your job or finances or family. Most people believe they should be in total control of most of their lives, especially their internal lives. Have you ever told a friend "Don't be angry" or "Don't be sad?" Can you maintain complete control over when your anger or sadness comes up for you? Can you truly control your memories and associations and reactions? Can you keep your life or your emotions "together," no matter what happens?

Of course you can't. It's impossible to control your memories. It's impossible to control your *reactions*. It's impossible to control your life. Period. But there is hope! I will say this next part as plainly as I possibly can. One of the few things we can control is how we treat ourselves. Can you control what others think of you? No. Can you control what happens to you? Not often. Can you control who gives you a chance or who doesn't? No. Can you control who will date you *or* where you'll get a job? No. Sure, you might have some say in these things, and you can often ask for what you want. I certainly recommend doing what you want if and when you have the ability, the money, the time, and the strength to do it. But can you control life?

One of the few things we can control is how we treat ourselves.

No. And this idea of having to have your life all together puts a specific unfair responsibility on you. It puts an unfair *weight* on you. This idea of having to have your life together makes you responsible for the outcomes of your life. And that is especially unfair because there is so much you can't control all by yourself. Having your life together (or trying to) is a lonely place to live. We've already talked about the importance of community and building spaces for yourself. And you know that this is possible. Instead of having your life together in that lonely place, where it all comes down to you, you could have a life that's intertwined with a community of good-hearted people. But of course, you're going to have to give up on the idea of you controlling your life or having it all together in the way your parents may have told you is best. You'll have to give up your beliefs around what makes you worthy or makes you productive, or what makes you "together."

Let's Stop and Think for a Moment

What does it mean to have your life "together"? When someone has it all together, how do they act? What words do they use? BONUS: How do you treat yourself when it's clear you don't have your life together?

The realization that I don't have to have my life together, now or ever, came just in time for me. For a while, people thought I represented all nonbinary people, and I hated it. It was a few years ago. Because I was famous online and the only prominent nonbinary person on Vine,

I kept getting emails from the media. They wanted quotes and interviews. They tried to find out what being nonbinary "really" was. Especially during pride month! They wanted to chat. And I loved the attention because I love attention, but I didn't love the pressure to represent nonbinary people correctly. I didn't realize it right away, but I was putting the pressure on myself. You see, I cared. I knew that I was likely the first nonbinary person many people saw or heard from.

I might be the first person they see who is not a man and not a woman. And when I first became well-known, I knew that there were many people like me. I knew them, and I knew of them, and I felt like I didn't want to let them down. I wanted to say the best things, the perfect things. I always wanted to say anything that would help push our movement forward and convince people who hate us that we are okay humans, and we are lovely and charming. It was a great ambition, except when it didn't work.

I tried to be a "perfect example of a nonbinary person" for a long time by pretending that I had my life together. At the time, many people believed a stereotype that nonbinary folks were mentally unstable or flat-out mentally ill. And the association of mental illness with gender-exciting people (i.e., trans or gender nonconforming or visibly queer or gender-fantastic people) is not new in Western culture, but it's especially prevalent in internet comments. The association used to upset me because there is no correlation, of course. The only relationship, perhaps, is that as trans people and nonbinary people, we get treated horribly, which is very hard on us. To be constantly disrespected is mentally taxing. To have to live in a society that ignores us and is so cruel to us is stressful.

As far as an automatic or natural connection between mental health difficulties and being nonbinary, it doesn't work that way. But at the time, it was a common assumption about us, and I thought it was my responsibility to seem like the sanest and most put-together person possible. And I thought that that was the best way to represent nonbinary people. And then, one day, I woke up. I realized that if anyone believes that a single person represents an entire group, that person is in more trouble than I can help them out of. If someone believes that I represent all nonbinary people and that all nonbinary people have my same experience, that person is deluding themselves, and they're not paying very close attention. And to be completely frank and up-front, I no longer feel like it's my job to make sure that non-trans people accept all nonbinary people. I don't feel it's necessary to "represent" us correctly. I bring this up because I bet you sometimes feel put in the spotlight in the worst way. You may not feel like you represent a larger group, but I bet you feel like you may be unfairly judged. You might be feeling the pressure I felt to have it all together.

> **If anyone believes that a single person represents an entire group, that person is in more trouble than I can help them out of.**

As someone who is now completely up-front about showing nonbinary life behind the scenes and vlogging nonbinary existence, let me tell you something. When I make a mistake, I might wish I hadn't, but I ultimately believe I should have the space to make a mistake. Over the years,

Unpredictability is part of the true beauty of life.

it's gotten so much easier. I drop the feeling of any pressure to seem like I have it all together. I don't want you to feel that pressure, ever. I don't want you to spend all your time trying to impress an image on others that you have your life together. I want you to stop trying to get your life together. All of life is essentially unpredictable. And that unpredictability is part of the true beauty of life. Unpredictability is part of the essence of why we're here. And if you can learn to surf the unpredictable and learn to enjoy those natural waves, you'll have an easy charm and magnetism, and your beauty will shine through. You will inspire others instead of trying to impress them. I've watched it happen. I've won many people over, people who've hated my guts. And part of the way I do it is in giving up on *trying* to win them over. So, instead, I just started telling the truth.

Just stop the attempt to be perfect. We all have hopes for ourselves, and we all make plans, and we all try our best, but things often go differently than we wish. It's okay to grieve when that happens. It's okay to be sad or angry about it, but it is not okay to judge yourself for not meeting an invisible standard. I was unhappy for years because I had hopes and plans and the world didn't match my ideals. I waited for years for the perfect man to love me. I waited for years to be a star on Broadway. What was I specifically waiting for? Not necessarily those exact things. I was waiting for those things to happen to make me happy. I was waiting for my life to begin. I was waiting to feel like I had it all together and that my life was on track because I had made the "right" choices.

I thought, *When I get what I want, I'll be satisfied.* In my childhood, I learned to live in a constant mode of yearning and stress, always on edge, always waiting for a shoe to drop or a fantasy to rescue me. I spent a lot of time escaping to an imaginary world where I was the right, perfect, together person. And as an adult, I spent years still living my whole life that way. My childhood trained me into yearning, and dropping the habit was nearly impossible. But I eventually found a way.

For years, I felt trapped. I thought if I could just get that man, if I could just get that job, if I could just get that money, if I could seem like I had it all together and somehow control my outside circumstances and get what I wanted, I could *then* relax. Then I could be happy. To break that mind habit, I had to do something drastic. I moved to the woods and hung out with a bunch of Buddhists. I completely let go of trying to hold myself together and I studied Zen for over twenty years.

Let's Stop and Think for a Moment

How do you live in an imaginary future? Do you sometimes let your dreams mean more to you than enjoying your present? It is important to honor your dreams, but could you put some future dream energy into your life today?

Part of what I learned during my time at the monastery was that I have no enthusiasm for a life that needs to be "together." I am not responsible for the best or the worst or the biggest or the "togetherest" life. I'm not responsible for "winning over" a man. I'm not responsible for getting the part after an audition. I'm not responsible for getting the job after an interview. I'm not responsible for learning how to be wealthy. I'm not responsible for having my life together before being happy. The only thing I'm responsible for is permitting myself to enjoy being comfortable whenever happiness visits me.

I gave up on wanting my life to be together a very long time ago. I gave up on wanting to impress other people a long time ago. I gave up on wanting that man, that career, that shit-together life filled with unhappiness. The time has come for you to give up on that.

And giving it up comes with the gift of the unpredictable. It's within those unpredictable moments where joy is found. Always trying to have your life together will put you in a constant state of unhappiness. As you read this, will you try something? You aren't expecting this, but please close your eyes, take three slow breaths, and give yourself permission to feel happy. Feel happy no matter what is happening in your life. Do this, for real, right now.

If you didn't do it—if you didn't try closing your eyes and breathing—why is that? Was there a voice in your head telling you not to do it? I would watch that voice very, very closely. When people think about giving up on having their life together and just letting life guide them, their fears can get in their way.

Sure, there may be people who have it worse than you in this life. There may be situations on earth that need our attention and participation for justice and equality, yes. But I'm telling you, even with all that being true, you can be happy. Even *before* you attempt to resolve those things, you can be kind to yourself in real time. We're together here, and you can be self-kind *before* you are anything close to your idea of together or perfect.

The real problem with getting *your* life together is that no one's life is together, and no one's life could ever be together because "together" is a standard that doesn't exist. Whatever "having your life together" means to you, it's something your parents gifted you. It may also be something capitalism gifted you, but it's not an ultimate truth of human life. The image of a "together life" is not even accurate or consistent from one person to another.

Furthermore, for most of us, "together" is a standard that keeps *changing*. As you grow, the definition of having your life together shifts focus. At first, it could mean the perfect relationship. But then, a few years later, it's the perfect job. And then, a few years after that, it's the money. And then it's the acclaim, and on and on. The goalposts keep shifting. And to be honest, having your life together always looks like the life you don't have. So you end up never appreciating the life you *do* have. The people you have in your life now, the job you have now, the love that you have right now, you never get to appreciate it if you're always trying for something else, always trying and seeking because you don't have your life "together" yet. Getting out

Having your life together always looks like the life you don't have.

of that mindset is one of the trickiest spiritual growth achievements you will ever encounter.

If you watch it for five minutes, if you watch the idea of "having it together" in your mind, you will watch the standards for "together" shift depending on whatever context is present in your life. You can feel like you're trying very hard to have your life together when it comes to your bank account. And then it'll shift over to the relationship with your mom; you need to try hard there too. And then it'll shift over to the way your boss treats you—try hard there. And then it'll shift over to the truths in this book. You're reading, and the goalposts keep moving back.

The goalposts never get close enough for you to kick the football between them. (I have no idea if that metaphor was correct, but I hope you get the idea. I don't know anything about sports, but the point I'm getting at is they're always beyond your reach.) So you can't ever get it together. Especially if what "together" means keeps changing. If you can free yourself from trying to have some kind of perfect life, you can also free yourself from wanting to seem perfect to other people. Then you can enjoy the unpredictability of life.

You can laugh. You can admit that something didn't go the way you planned. You can say, "Whoops," and you can make it into a charming, lovely moment of the only actual "together," in-the-moment honesty. The connections humans have between each other, that's a togetherness. Let's be together. Let's roll with life together. However it goes, let's enjoy how deeply we are connected. And let's give up on trying to have our life together in the way our family told us is correct. Because if we can give that up, we can be free. And you deserve that. You deserve to roll with the life you've got and not answer to an imaginary parent in your head.

Let's Stop and Think for a Moment

Write down some parenting tips for the voices in your head. Feel free to give that voice in your head that demands you have it all together a new focus. Tell that voice, in no uncertain terms, that you are not living to impress it. Can you imagine having a life where that inner voice is irrelevant?

You deserve to flow with the unexpected and not "have it all together" or have "good excuses" for existing. You deserve the chance to face bullies unarmed with the perfect answer but carrying a quiver of self-dignity. You deserve unprepared adventures.

I Put the News in Newsmax

When a producer gave me the chance to speak on a huge platform—national TV—I had no clue what I would say. I thought, *I'm really LGBTQ. I'm still that poor queer kid from Nowhere, Pennsylvania. My life is a mess. I make videos and dance around. Don't I really need to get my life together to be on TV?* I didn't feel like I had the *authority* to speak on much of anything. All I really knew about was the self-love that had become the focus of my life. But that was "California woo-woo stuff," as my mother would always say. I needed to present an image. I needed to be polished and super articulate to be on a news show. And I didn't feel like I was either of those things. I wasn't even sure of what I wanted to say. If a TV show wanted to talk about my first book, *How to Be You*, and its self-love stories, the book and whatever I had to say had better be good. I better have it all together. I thought, *You can't just go on TV unless your book is a big success.* Thank goodness it was about to be a success. But I didn't know that yet.

I didn't know—or even guess—that it would be a success, honestly. I poured my heart into that book. And I didn't know if it would sell one copy to my friend's grandma or no copies at all. But I wanted to get some things out of my heart and on paper so that I wouldn't feel so alone. And I wanted other people not to feel so alone. I never write to be "brilliant" or to sound like I know everything. Through my time at the monastery and through growing up in that isolated rural town in Pennsylvania, I had learned what was most important to me. But when TV called, I didn't know if what I had learned would be "enough."

I had learned how to be myself without shame. I had learned how to be in love with myself without hesitation and hiding. And all I wanted to do was get that into a book and share it with the world. I had no idea if it would resonate as deeply as I wanted with people. But it ended up resonating so deeply, in fact, that conservative cable news would notice. Penguin Random House published the book in 2016, and I had been out for a few years as a nonbinary public figure, using they/them pronouns. And there were very few of us nonbinary public figures. I must have been very high in the Google search results! Newsmax emailed me. When I got the email from the producers on this conservative network, I didn't realize I would be the first nonbinary person to be out and proud and telling my story on national television, period.

So, I said yes to Newsmax's email. I didn't know if it would sell books, but I felt a national TV platform to share my mission and message would be too good to pass up. I certainly didn't feel like I had my life together enough to be in front of a national audience, but I knew what was in my heart. If I'm going to spread a message of love, kindness, and acceptance, I thought, why not take every opportunity to do it? It seemed like a good idea, but the day I ended up in a studio in front of the cameras, I was nervous as heck. I certainly wasn't cool and collected like I thought I should be.

We filmed the segment in the middle of a weekday. I took the subway from the East Village, where Jeff and I were living at the time, to Midtown Manhattan, where the Newsmax TV studios were. And I remember making great friends with the makeup artist. She was kind, she had a beautiful laugh, and we gossiped and had fun and picked out lashes together. And she put me at ease. I said to her under my breath, very quietly, "Can I ask you something?" "Yes," she said. "Why do you work here?" She laughed, her head tilting back. "They pay me to be here," she said. As you might have guessed, I was nervous about the maybe-combative interview and my first appearance on national TV. My new friend finished my makeup, and the producer of the show I was going to be on came over to introduce herself. She escorted me onto the set.

And there was Dennis, the program's host, sitting behind his desk. He was at home in this hostile place. He was in charge, and there I was, a mess. It was a typical cable news set, with a big screen behind him and an unused pencil jar on the desk in front of him. And I saw my chair; I would sit on the other side of the desk from the host. I remember thinking the producers meant

us to look like opposing forces. He was cool and together, and I was queer and messy. But I had something
going for me: I knew I would be kind to myself no matter how the interview went. I knew I would be literally
saying kind things to myself throughout the whole
thing. I knew I wouldn't rehash how it went or whether
my message was ultimately "together enough." I knew
that a couple hours after the interview, I would be kind
to myself, as I had committed to be kind to myself always.

Also, Dennis didn't know that I had been taught at
the monastery to try to move beyond being an opposing
force. I didn't know that would be handy on a TV set.
My teacher at the monastery taught me how to interact
with opposing people without opposing them back. I
was taught to *not* become an equal and opposite force
to anyone who approached me with anger or accusations or hate. My teacher talked about "asking them to
nail Jell-O to a wall." Don't help a hater by becoming
the force they want to fight with. Don't offer resistance.
Don't offer what they want.

What an opposing hateful party generally desires is
an equal or attempted equal pushback. And if you
gracefully turn to Jell-O in front of them, if you don't
oppose, if you react with kindness, any opposing-force
person will expend all their energy in frustration. They
will be unable to push you around if their pushes melt
into the movement you are making already. If you are
not someone who cares about being gotten, they won't

be able to play gotcha. Far from having the perfect answers, I would have the loving and kind answers. Maybe that would be enough.

Newsmax had filled the segment before mine with "experts" in nonbinary identity. I put "experts" in quotes because the four people on the "expert panel" were not nonbinary. They didn't even seem to be LGBTQ. They seemed like they had it all together. They knew all the right things to say to a conservative audience about us, but they weren't being honest—they couldn't know what it was really like to be me. They were a group of cisgender people on a cable news panel to discuss nonbinary people and how odd, how selfish, how *liberal*, and how awful college kids are because they force their professors to use "weird" pronouns. That was always meant to be the lead-in to me.

And before and during the filming of my segment, I had no idea that that panel would even be broadcast before I spoke. The show evidently meant for me to represent a liberal wackiness, an out-there-ness. I was supposed to be an expert myself, on the "other side." I walked into that studio and, for a national audience, I said, "I'm not a man, I'm not a woman. I use 'they' pronouns. My name is Jeffrey." I tried to be charming if not polished and together. I thought I could do my part to force the LGBTQ-phobes of the world to nail Jell-O to the wall. Maybe I could transmogrify some of the world's hate into a more valuable creature: an expansion of what it means to be human.

From the very first moment we met, Dennis, the host, was extremely disrespectful, and I decided to turn on the charm extra for him. I decided to be witty and as cute as I could be. And I also decided to do a very LGBTQ thing: I had to make sure he would respect my pronouns, but instead of just plainly stating how to respect me, I made my request for dignity into a charming, quaint little joke. At least, I *thought* it was adorable. I looked at Dennis. "I just want to make sure your teleprompter is correct," I said, smiling. "Oh, I'm sure someone on my team has told you that I use they/them pronouns. When you're doing the introduction, you wanna say things like, '*They* are amazing. They have written the best-selling book. They are gorgeous.' You know, things like that." I wanted to seem like I had it all together and that we could laugh like old buddies. What was I thinking? The nervousness was getting to me, I guess. And I started laughing. Dennis did not. He turned to me and said, his voice almost a growl, "I talk how I talk. If I say the wrong thing, you'll have to correct me on air." I felt utterly alone and very all over the place. And *ding*! The red light on the top of the camera turned on, and we were filming. *I love you, Jeffrey. Thank you for doing this. It's okay to feel whatever you feel. I am with you,* I said to myself inside my head.

I took a breath and loved myself. All the Buddhist training rose up in me and I forgot to pretend I had it all together. I was the first nonbinary person to discuss being us on national TV, and any pressure melted away. As I talked out loud to Dennis, I kept talking to me. *You*

don't need to be anything other than you. I love you.
That interview, to me, was filled with love mainly because I talked to myself kindly during the whole thing. I
focused on the kindness. That interview is one of the
proudest moments of my life. That host disrespected me
as a person, and maybe he even hated me without knowing me. But the whole thing taught me a valuable lesson:
If he can hate me without knowing me, if so many people
can hate me, that means that I can love anyone and everyone without knowing them.

What may be interesting to note is that conservatives
follow me on social media to this day. I guess a lot of
people are drawn to someone telling an unvarnished,
not-put-together truth, even if it comes from someone
they might not have considered listening to before. I
think my conservative following grew out of that particular Newsmax appearance and some of the things I have
said. I also think my surprising conservative audience follows me because of my commitment to kindness. I hope
that's why everyone follows me! I may not always have
my life "together," but I never stop telling the truth. I
never stop being open or bold about who I am or where
I'm coming from, and I also never purposefully try to
make people feel bad or guilty. If you take a look through
the analytics of the people who follow me on social media, you'll see that about a third are self-identified conservatives and Republicans, and a third are Democrats and
liberals. And a third haven't said or are independents. It's
people of all ages and from all walks of life.

Can I be totally honest? I used to think I'd done something wrong to have conservatives following me. I thought maybe they were hate watching, to see someone fall apart under the pressure of being hated online and in society. Were they sticking around to hate on me themselves? I found the breakdown of my followers' political beliefs troubling because conservatives, particularly conservative Christians in the United States, have been very cruel to me and people like me. And somehow, it also felt like it was in some way betraying the people who might be following me for reasons that would open their hearts. But who am I to tell people who they should follow? Maybe I have some kind of appeal to people, even though they are conservative. My fear and concern have mellowed over the years.

And today, I even see it all as a badge of honor. I see my conservative fan base as an outgrowth of the fact that I tell the truth and tell it without fear. And I think people can recognize that I will be plain with them, no matter where they came from or what else they may believe.

I can love Newsmax viewers and love people like you reading this. I can be messy and so can you. We can all not have our lives or our sentences together, and we can be just fine. We can relax. I can love you, reader, even if we've never met. I have received many messages and DMs over the years from people who saw that interview and fell in love with their own self-respect, which they saw reflected in me.

So, with that in mind, with you in mind, I have felt a deep sense of belonging ever since that interview. I have felt free to not be presenting an image to others. I can present me. I can be messy and I can belong. Also, if I can belong within myself, speak for myself, and tell my truth in that hostile instance and in that anti-Jeffrey place, I can tell my truth anywhere, and I can tell it as unpolished and as confusing as it needs to be. I can be with myself anywhere if I can be with myself sitting in that interview chair facing Dennis and a bank of cameras. I just kept saying to myself, *Thank you. I'm glad you're here. I love you very much. You're doing great. I'm with you. I'm not going anywhere.* You don't need to know what you're doing. None of us do. You don't need to have it all together, but you need to be kind to yourself and continue to speak your truth.

KEY TAKEAWAYS

1. You cannot wait for happiness or perfection. Life rarely "comes together," and you don't need to be "together" yourself.

2. Unpredictability is part of the true beauty of life.

3. You don't constantly need a reason, schedule, or agenda to justify your existence. Find a centered life in the things that bring you joy.

Chapter 8

Stop Trying to Avoid Your Pain and Start Wearing Your Pain as a Badge of Honor

My Sex Life

Jeff and I have revolutionized our sex lives. Again. There have been several studies linking a painful childhood with difficulty being free to express yourself sexually. Add to that the pain of being LGBTQ and hiding it for all of my young life. And add the pain of knowing people who died of AIDS. Sex, to me, has been a difficult, traumatic, and painful journey. Jeff and I have been monogamous for the decade plus that we've been together. I had no idea the many blind spots and spiritual growth moments I had waiting for me in our marriage. I had no idea the unhealed pain that would bubble up in our relationship.

I remember as a teen, I just wanted a boy to rescue me from my pain. Growing up with my mom as an example—I identified with my mom more than my dad—I saw that she hadn't precisely chosen wisely in her relationship with my dad. My parents had a tumultuous, agonizing, angry marriage. I always remember them fighting and getting in digs at each other. I suspect that my parents never got a divorce because, like abortion, divorce was just off the table for religious reasons. Watching them was painful.

They fought over and over. Loud big fights and snide under-the-breath side-comment fights. From my perspective, it always seemed like they didn't like each other. And that was the only example I had of love and marriage, an arduous example. In a rip-roaring fight, my mom once said, "Keep going, and you'll get none of what you got last night." I was around ten years old, and I had no clue what she meant. Now I know. Sex was leverage. Sex was a tool with which to pick fights and inflict pain. I was to carry the burdensome baggage of religious trauma, childhood trauma, and an example of a painful marriage until way past my time of healing through my work at the monastery. At the monastery, we're celibate. We work on other things. I didn't realize it was all related.

For years, I thought I was a prude or just didn't like sex. But actually, I was attracted to people all the time. I just had incredible anxiety about doing it with anyone. The LGBTQ stereotype can be that we're wild and sexually free, but that wasn't the case for me. I had sex for the first time in college, and it was embarrassing and stressful, and altogether awkward. It was painful because it wasn't "working," and neither of us knew what we were doing. And we both bought into the idea that we *should* know what we were doing.

And that's why I'm grateful for Jeff. I never knew I would find someone so wonderful that my pain could be an integrated part of our lives together. I never knew I could talk about my nervousness and self-inflicted pressure with a caring and accepting partner. I never knew I could bring my whole self—even the sensitive, painful parts of me—into a sexual relationship. Jeff and I communicate, and we both ask for what we want. Being with him has been the gift of my life in many ways, but especially in the bedroom. I recently asked him if we could spend more time naked and together *without* having sex. And we do. We just spend time intimately and kindly with each other without a "goal" in mind. I was surprised that he wanted that too. So, I was glad I said it.

Pain Is Not a Problem

I'm sorry for your pain. Your pain is beautiful. You didn't deserve what happened to you, but what happened to you has made you, at least partly, into the beautiful person you are today. It's important to note that you deserve both sympathy and kindness around everything hard that has happened to you, but you also deserve a feeling of empowerment around your past. I detest when people say, "I learned so much from my trauma. It was a great life lesson, what happened to me." Listen, life is not about learning lessons. Life is not about

Your pain will heal when you embrace your history in a compassionate way.

getting something out of what happens to us. I think far too many people learn something to intellectualize and make sense of something that was totally out of their control. When I say, "I'm sorry for your pain," I mean any of your pain. I mean, I'm sorry for the psychic pain of having any of the difficult times you've had. It is essential that you understand that those things should not have happened to you. You didn't deserve any of it. *And* the pain of your past is something that you can integrate. Your pain will heal when you embrace your history in a compassionate way. You can even start to celebrate the you that you've become as a result of those things. That is a very healthy, happy, and beautiful approach for those of us who have had a difficult life.

It probably sounds odd when I say that you can begin to celebrate your pain. Aren't we supposed to run from pain? What I mean is that your pain has taught you the most profound sense of empathy for all human beings, and because of that, you can wear your pain as a badge of honor. Some people are traumatized as kids, and they become total jerks—or worse, some people are traumatized as kids and they take it out on everyone they meet every single day for the rest of their lives.

Let's Stop and Think for a Moment

Tell yourself about your pain. Take a moment to consider or write down some of your terrible, no-good, painful moments. I know you don't want to consider this, but the possibility of freedom is important. Focus your thoughts on who you were at the time these things happened. Does that version of you deserve to be acknowledged? Thanked? Encouraged? Celebrated?

But you are different. You are the kind of person who makes choices **Your pain is *not* your shame.** to transcend some of the pain you've been through. You have grown up to be highly enthusiastic about helping other people feel accepted. Because of the painful experiences you went through, your pain is part of the map of the beautiful, empathetic person you are today. I'm guessing being unjustly or harshly punished at a young age taught you that you should hide your pain. I'm thinking your family system taught you that your pain is a shame that you carry with you. I know society taught you to keep your pain covered by a persona of being the "perfect person." Should I go on? Your pain is *not* your shame. Your pain is the gateway that has helped you to feel compassion for the pain of others. It is handy for spiritual growth because compassion for others can teach you to feel sympathy for yourself. Your pain can guide you to be a person who is devoted to kindness to everyone. That is part of your life story. That is part of the road map of how you became a bighearted person. And that bigheartedness should be celebrated with gusto.

From a purely philosophical perspective, we can't know who you would be if those things had not happened to you. But we sure know who you are today. You are a caring person, a deeply devoted person who loves other people and creatures with an innocent and open heart. You are a person who cares. It's time to admit that and to celebrate it. And the relationship between your caring and what you've been through is that those experiences have given you perspective. It's the perspective necessary to feel the pain of others and devote your life to *minimizing* the pain of others. What you went through, the pain you felt, the reactions you had, any ways you were compensating to avoid your pain, and any ways you were covering up your pain, none of that is your fault. You don't have to own any of that. But I *would* ask you to own your full humanity. Own the fact that you are the kind of person who has certain reactions because you went through difficult things. Embrace that fact about yourself.

You *are* the kind of person who has reactions and patterns and sometimes difficult emotions because you have faced difficult things. You're a tapestry. You're a walking poetry of complications. You're an emblem of what it means to be a whole, complex human being. And so it's worth considering: Can you be at peace with your pain? I'm going to go out on a limb and say that if a person one day realizes (through therapy, through coaching, through a book) that they are in a great deal of emotional pain, the first thing that happens is they try to hide the pain. People try to pretend they don't have hurt. They feel bad that they have it. They try to get rid of it. They try to fix it. Almost everybody goes through some version of those steps.

What I want you to do is be fully at peace with the pain as it is. Don't try to change your emotional discomfort. Don't try to fix it, don't try to minimize it, and certainly don't feel ashamed about it. Your pain comes from something you couldn't control. It was something others did to you. You had no choice then, but you have a choice now. You can choose to embrace who you were when the trauma was happening. You can choose to welcome and accept who you were if you spent time compensating for, hiding, and minimizing your pain. Some of us have tried to do that for years. And that's not a problem! And you can choose to embrace who you are now; you are the person who sees all this pain, and you are the person who is ready to be grateful that who you are today is compassionate to yourself and to others.

Let's Stop and Think for a Moment

Hold a pain party. Invite friends if you'd like. Give yourself gifts. Take some time to acknowledge all you've survived and how it has made you feel. Eat snacks and make decorations for your personal commemoration of your past. Celebrate your survival skills and your commitment to being happy today. What does your pain party look like?

If you celebrate your pain, if you shamelessly embrace that the pain in your past is a part of who you are, if you stop running from or trying to hide your pain, you will be a beacon of possibility for others. I make videos all the time where I talk about my pain and painful experiences. I don't hide the fact that I'm in pain sometimes. That's very odd for social media. It's very *different*. There is toxic positivity on the internet, and I will make videos where I'm far from positive. I'll make videos where I am showing my pain. There is no mitigation in these videos. There is no filter and no minimizing, and no thought given to how I look. As far as I can tell from the beautiful, loving comments I get, these videos are a relief for people. You can experience this level of relief too when you embrace your pain without shame. You can celebrate your ability to feel and be vulnerable. When you're not running from your pain, you're here. You're present. If you're not running from your pain, you can address anything that you need to in order to bring kindness into your life. If you are not running, you can be your whole self, your fully integrated self, who feels happy and sad and everything else without shame. Pain is not a problem because feelings are not a problem. Reactions are not a problem. Who you were and who you are because you have these beautiful reactions is not a problem either.

When I was at the monastery and looking at the pain that has been a big part of my life, the pain felt more significant than me. The Buddhist tradition that I studied does not mention past lives, and we don't talk about having been someone in a past life who is different from your present self. It is not a tradition of talking about anything beyond what is here and now. I bring this experience up because at the monastery, we would sit facing a blank wall and meditate—sometimes for hours a day. And I would have these waves of sad, grief-filled pain come over me; the emotional pain would almost physically take over my entire body. I realized that the pain felt like it was *more than just mine*. That was a wonderful feeling. It was a bit of a relief because it felt like I didn't have to own pain that was bigger than myself. Although I have no clue whether past lives exist, my pain felt like it was the culmination—the pain culmination of several lifetimes. It felt like my pain was as big as the universe, which was a relief.

I saw a direct connection between all the swirling, huge pain I felt and the cruelty of any human being to another. I had a perspective on the pain that many human beings carry. I felt the connection between humans and the relationship between the world and me. In that moment of realization, I also embraced the fact that my attempts to avoid my pain were a good thing too. I wasn't ready.

I had a harrowing childhood. I used to deflect, distract, and cover up all my pain. I tried to get away from my pain or pretend it wasn't there. I had all these compensations and avoidances to help me survive. With those waves of pain at the monastery came a wave of gratitude that I did the best that I could to stay present to myself in the only way I knew how. I also realized that distracting myself from my pain was not the same as freedom. Pretending I wasn't grieving over the happy childhood that I could have had was not the same as having a happy adulthood. When I went away to the monastery, I assumed I was going there to be, y'know . . . Buddhist . . . Zen, peaceful, emotionless, robotically "above it all." What I realized pretty quickly through Buddhist training was that the opposite was true.

I didn't go to a monastery to diminish the Jeffrey I had been and become a "clean" or better version of a human being. I didn't go to a monastery to *downplay* my personality and *"upplay"* a zen, calm image. Spiritual practice taught me to *feel more*, care more, and be in pain more. Spiritual practice led me to be more Jeffrey. Not to escape Jeffrey, but to always be more of myself. And that would be a life lesson that came to me early and has stayed with me for my entire life.

My First Shave

I have no idea where I got the idea itself. Probably I wanted to look like a Rockette. I wanted beautifully smooth legs from hip to formerly hairy toe. In today's language, and from today's perspective, I could talk about gender dysphoria. And I could talk about me as a teenager, wanting to express all the gender, wishing to embody the wheelbarrows of gender that had rolled around with me since as far back as I could remember. But back then, when I was sixteen, I just couldn't stand having hairy legs anymore. I wanted that smooth-leg look. And the only problem I had was figuring out how to do so much shaving all by myself. It's one of those interesting traumatized-kid places, but it also strikes me as an LGBTQ place. Without any guidance, stuck on a farm, so profoundly alone in those woods, it was just me facing my very hairy legs. And this was long before Google, so I couldn't even ask the internet for assistance. But I was nothing if not determined and enthusiastic. And even then, I was nothing if not diligent and good at solving problems. Still, it took me a long time to shave.

The only thing I could find in the house was a disposable razor with a single blade. It still had the tiny plastic blade-protecting cap on it. If you've ever attempted to shave something with a 1990s disposable safety razor, you know that they're not the easiest and not the best. And I had *one* of them, and I wanted two smooth legs from top to bottom. It was challenging and slow. It took a very long time. My toes got all prune-y, and I nicked my legs in several places, but I kept at it. I kept squirting shampoo on my hairy legs, rubbing it around, and hacking through the leg hair jungle. I remember the water getting cold, and I remember the drain under the spigot—the metal plate with holes in it—clogging over and over with my natural hairiness. And I also remember feeling deeply alone. I was elated and scared. Happy and nervous. I think I clogged my throat with emotion. But I wanted what I wanted. And even though I assumed I would get in trouble—even though I knew if people looked and noticed that I had smooth legs, they would hate my guts, they would discriminate, they would make fun of me at school; even though I knew my father would be angry—I stayed as focused as possible. Somehow. I still knew that I had to do what I had set out to do.

I cleaned myself up afterward, as best as I could. I didn't even know the trick (no one had taught me to shave my face either) where you use little bits of tissue to stop bleeding. My legs were bleeding in a few places, and I had missed shaving patches of hair here and there. Honestly, I probably looked a mess, but my father had knocked a few times during the procedure, two muscular pounds on the door. And I suspected that he suspected something was going on. It took forever, and I felt rushed the whole time. I loved having smooth legs and I was stressed for *anyone* to know. My father knew something was up, and my protestations of "nothiiiiing" from inside the bathroom didn't turn him off from his parental instincts that something was very wrong.

Throughout my life, I've always had a bold streak that tempered the sadness and feelings of loneliness. My fears have always been in tension with my rebellious spirit. And this situation was no different. I didn't know what would happen, but I had to do my thing. And with shaving and expressing my gender, I had gotten to such a point of desperation that part of me honestly didn't care what would happen. I had to be free. So, after I finished shaving my legs, with the pain and the bleeding, I put on the shortest shorts I owned, and I even made them shorter with a roll or two.

Looking back, maybe part of me hoped that Mom and Dad would notice and that this could be an excuse to talk about who I am. I wanted to tell my truth. I wanted to talk about what I wanted in life, where I was trying to go, and why. And oh boy, Dad noticed. He said, "What are those?" He pointed at my legs with a look on his face that mixed disgust with humor. And I can't remember exactly, but I'm guessing I said something sarcastic. Sarcasm would be my defensive shield even after my teenage years. I probably said, "These are my legs. Aren't they gorgeous?" I may not remember my words exactly, but I do remember Dad's reaction. Dad went *ballistic*. I had seen him do it before, but this seemed to be on a new level. He seemed like a different person. It wasn't my typical angry dad. It also wasn't the dad from church. It wasn't the dad from Thanksgiving. It wasn't the dad from driving me to Boy Scouts. Something came over him. And that was that. He got physical, and he got violent. He was a swinging, unpredictable embodiment of rage. As he was hitting me, I remember that I wished the queerness would leave my body. I wished I could stop the violence by letting my queerness go. I imagined the rainbow essence of my LGBTQ-ness hitting the wall behind me as fists hit my face. I imagined a gooey rainbow of my sparkled soul sliding down the wall behind me. But thankfully, the rainbow sparkle was too strong. It would not and could not leave me no matter how hard I wished it away.

It felt like the fists were for ridding me of my LGBTQ-ness, to knock the queerness out of my body. The fists wanted me to be the perfect son—the son that wasn't an embarrassment. I desperately wanted to be a hollow shell that would be filled with his dreams and stuffed with his ideas of what a child should offer to a parent. And even in the moment, I remember having a split soul. I remember it happening to me—I remember him beating me, but I also remember the feeling of watching it all from above, from across the room, from a distance. And that idea of my beautiful glittery rainbow queerness hitting the wall as my father hit me has stayed with me. Dad's fists left a mark that day.

Afterward, I felt much younger than sixteen. I felt like a child caught playing the wrong kind of dress-up. One good thing to come out of that day was that it taught me that nobody would ever knock out my rainbow essence. I learned that the queerness of who I am couldn't leave me, no matter what I or anyone else did. In a sense, the pain of that moment, both physical and emotional, helped me realize that pain is nothing to fear—that pain wouldn't change who I was. Of course,

I wouldn't wish that situation on anybody, but it did teach me that I could survive. I can talk about it. I can embrace it all. My father's fists taught me that hate is something I could survive.

"You Can't Talk About That"

I know that your parents may have told you that your pain is too much, that if you feel it all, you won't survive. I've been there myself. I have been terrified of my pain. I spent years trying, in various ways, to be a person who wasn't in pain. I made videos on the internet where I would only talk about positive things. All that toxic positivity was ultimately driven by fear. I never lied or presented an image that wasn't close to the genuine Jeffrey, but there were times when I thought, *Oh, I can't make a video about that. I can't talk about that. I can't be open about a painful subject because people will assume all trans people have mental health issues.* It was related to my gender and my core personhood. Obviously, there is no connection between being trans and having mental health issues. (Unless you count that almost all of us are treated horribly from the time we're very young to the time we're an adult. Trust me—that can affect a person's emotional, mental, and even physical health.) But our trans pain is not, or at least should not be, automatic.

Today, when I film videos, my pain is obvious. I make videos where I celebrate my emotions—even my hurt. I make videos where my feelings are triumphant. Listen, I am extremely happy to be alive. I know this sounds odd, but I am grateful to express the full range of what I feel, including pain and compassion. I still carry the sensitivity I was mocked for as a child. And that's great to me. The softness visits me every day. It's something I celebrate. Today, I even get happy when that pain visits because I know it is all part of the story of how I became me. I understand that a very valid weight is part of the story of how I became an easily affected, and beautiful human being. I would ask you to embrace yourself in the same way.

I would ask you to be willing and allow your pain to visit from time to time.

I would ask you to acknowledge and allow the emotional pain into your life.

I would ask you to celebrate your pain as part of the beautiful, complicated tapestry of your life story. From the beginning, your life story is a painful, beautiful patchwork.

Let's Stop and Think for a Moment

Consider this. If you had a friend who was in emotional pain, how would you treat them? What would you say to them? What advice would you give to a friend who was experiencing some of the pain you yourself have been through?

On Feeling Broken

It is crystal clear to me that you are not broken. I think people say that and use that word to refer to a kind of loss of innocence. You're young, running around okay, and then a significant, maybe painful, life event happens. You spiritually wake up to how painful and awful life can be. Using the word *broken* seems like a mistake. That time of life, when a big, painful thing happens, can also be beautiful and an excuse to grow more significant than you ever thought possible.

Broken implies you're like a teacup or a car engine. You need "fixing," or maybe the problem is that you can't fix yourself at all. You've been walking through life assuming you can't fix yourself because you're bad at fixing, or maybe you're just so broken that fixing yourself is impossible. There's not enough spiritual glue to put your broken-teacup self back together again.

As a metaphor, *broken* captures the fact that there are life events that change us forever. It also speaks to the idea that there is no going back to how you used to be. There is no way to stop growing and changing. But *broken* has negative connotations that suggest somehow that *not broken* or *whole* is better, or that *fixed* is better. I know precisely why it's been so hard for you to fix yourself. It's because you are not broken. You cannot fix something that isn't broken; it will never work.

See, "fixing" yourself is a mode that your parents taught you. Once you see, truly see, that you're magnificent and lovely as you are, it will be apparent that there is no possible way to fix yourself. I can hear you screaming as many people have screamed to me: "But I have a running list in my head of what's wrong with me!

I could give you the full report on what needs to be fixed!" That's fine. But that's not the same as broken. An inability to fix that stuff is not a problem at all. Some things live beyond fixing and exist more in the land of acceptance. So, the fact that society and your parents and whoever else taught you a list of what they thought were flaws is irrelevant.

And it's a distraction. Do you need to believe you're broken in order to change? Hell no! In my experience, lasting change comes only after we realize that nothing about us is wrong or broken. Self-kindness is the gateway to change. Kindness is the only vantage point where you can see what you're genuinely doing to yourself and others with any pattern. Kindness is

> **Lasting change comes only after we realize that nothing about us is wrong or broken.**

where you can feel the pain of hurting yourself and others with this dumpster full of unexamined childhood garbage. The garbage is not your fault! It doesn't make you broken! It makes you human and, rather nicely, it makes you beautiful. It sets you on your own hero's journey toward healing. If you want to stop any pattern of behavior that is causing you pain, you must see the beauty and the love in your heart first. It's the most pleasant way to transcend the difficult times from our childhood, and it's also the most effective.

I promise you that if you spend the rest of your life going over and over the list of what makes you broken, you will never heal. You will never "fix" yourself. You'll never be "unbroken." It is the way you see yourself that is the problem. The list of "wrong things about me" is the problem, not anything that's on the list! The only thing that is genuinely *broken* is this human system we have. Culture is broken if a good-hearted person like you grew up being taught that you need to be fixed.

KEY TAKEAWAYS

You are worth any effort. Period. You get to decide. Will your life be about others' reactions to you, implanted standards, and self-hate, or will you concentrate on healing?

Dear Little Jeffrey, Age Eighteen

My goodness, you are such a beautiful, free spirit. I know it doesn't feel that way, and I know it feels like a lot of people are against you, but by the time you're my age, forty-four, you'll get an email from someone from the junior class, the year below you. And this high school buddy, who you won't remember, will praise you for having come out in your senior year. This random email will bring you joy and closure about your high school experience. Senior year feels so chaotic for you—you feel like coming out is messy and that you should have your life together. And this new email friend, who you'll strike up a correspondence with, will tell you what your coming-out meant to him. He'll let you know how he couldn't come out as gay himself, how he thought maybe he never would, and how seeing you inspired him. He'll also tell you something bittersweet and painful. He'll say, "I'm so glad you came out because it took the heat off me. When you came out, you gave all of the bullies in our school a focal point. You gave them a place to direct their violence." When you read those words, your first reaction will be an angry feeling of unfairness. But of course, that was an attempt to deflect from our pain. It's a feeling you know well, a feeling that it's unjust that you had to take the heat. It's unfair because you chose to be honest with everyone at school and what you got was unkindness. That was a harrowing experience. And that pain will blossom into near-universal compassion later in your life. And it will be beautiful.

I wish I could be there to hug you and tell you that the heat that you're taking for being yourself is not your fault. I know you feel like you planned your decision to come out poorly. And yes, it was stumbly, bumbly, and fumbly. I know you feel (often) that you didn't make the right decision—that you didn't plan your coming-out well enough to "make sure" everyone understood and liked you. But their reaction isn't your fault. Please leave behind that self-judgment and those regretful feelings as soon as you can. I wish you could hear me now: I love you so much, and I admire you so much. We will learn to be proud of our pain. We will learn to be proud of the deep well of compassion that has sprung forth from our past pain. But of course, for you, that is present pain. As I look back from where I am now, I am shocked by your bravery. Inspired, yes, but also shocked that you told everyone who you are in that small and small-worldview Pennsylvania town. You told the school, your church, and your mom (three times!).

You're eighteen, and you blasted the hinges off your closet door, and that deserves celebrating. I don't understand how you had any context to come out, to this day. You've seen no LGBTQ people on TV, and you still told your truth. To be honest, it's something I draw inspiration from. In a way, your pain of being closeted was enough of a catalyst to begin a life of truth-telling. The pain has become something beautiful. You are someone I draw inspi-

ration from to this day. I know that you've been waiting since you were very young, waiting until you could get to college, to come out. I just have to say how happy I am that you didn't wait that extra year. I'm so delighted that you came out now, as a high school senior. I'm quite proud that you didn't worry about having your life together, that you didn't worry about having your narrative together. You didn't worry about the genuine possibility of rejection.

When facing some hateful folks, being able to stick with yourself and your truth is a skill we'll build on for years. I want to talk to you about something you've never shared with anyone in your entire life, and something that I've never shared with anyone either: You wished for a long time that your coming-out would get you rejected. It sounds strange. When you were a kid, you were treated horribly in many ways. And for many years, you hoped that when you came out, your family would reject you and that your LGBTQ identity would be an excuse for you to no longer have to have contact with them.

I want to let you know that I am not in contact with our family anymore. I made that decision primarily for you. One day recently, here at forty-four years old, I remembered that I wished so sincerely that my coming-out would cause my whole family to reject me. And that was a red flag. Oddly, I wanted to protect myself by being kicked out of my childhood home. I wished for that rejection because the family relationship wasn't healthy. Because I knew deep down, even at eighteen, that not being *in contact was the only appropriate answer for my mental and spiritual health.*

Jeffrey, you've lived a harrowing life already, and you have survived. You've lived through such pain, and you have endured. I want you to know that I love everything about the person you've become, the adult you are becoming, and I love what you want out of life. I often think back to you and how sure you are about justice and how I never expected that sureness and that clarity to go away for a few years. But it's okay. I am here remembering you and feeling sure about justice again. Today, I am driven by fairness, just like you. I praise you for being so passionate and crystal clear about who you are and what you deserve.

Your life has not been fair. What happened to you is not acceptable. What people did to you was not warranted. The pain you experienced as a kid and the pain you are experiencing now, at eighteen, is deeply unjust. You will think about and care about justice for your entire life, although you will try to avoid the pain of caring for many years. You will try to avoid the pain of injustice for many years. You will go through a time of trying to ignore the pain you feel and have felt. For years, you'll try to pretend your past didn't happen.

Part of the price that your family will want you to pay to be in that family is never talking about the pain you went through. We will eventually decide together, you and I, that denying the pain and avoiding the subject is too high a price to pay for any relationship. I'm so glad we decided that together, because being out of contact with our family is the best decision. I am happy that you have learned to thrive on unpredictability. Your childhood has been chaotic, and you're learning to hold your own space of predictability without sacrificing an open life. I am so glad that you feel the wiggles, the nonbinary flow of energy, so deep in your soul that you embody it daily.

I know you're still afraid of relationships and sex and that you want to get your life together with a partner and with a career. But I wish that you could savor the freedom found in the unpredictability of life for a little bit longer. I know that you won't even kiss anyone you want to kiss for a few years. (Sorry if that's surprising news.) But it's all okay. I know that not having love like that in your life will feel so empty, so lonely, and so unfair. I know that right now and for the next few years, a yearning for romantic love will be such a point of pain for you. But I also know that you are whole without romantic love. Every billboard, every TV commercial, tells you that you should be straight and have romantic love. And if you can't be straight and you can't have romantic love, you are less of a person. But you are a complete, whole, beautiful person. The life you've built and the honesty and integrity that flows through everything you choose to do are so poetically profound and beautiful. I know you get angry when Mom says, "You're just so brave. You've always been so brave." I know you want to scream back at her, "I shouldn't have to live in a world where I am so brave!" But of course you are brave.

In the near future, you will make the world that you want. You will help make a world where LGBTQ kids don't have to be so brave. You will help make a world where LGBTQ kids like you—I know you hate when I call you a kid . . . You will make a world where LGBTQ young adults like you don't have to be so brave. You will make a world where young adults who are LGBTQ have examples of people who are like them. You're going to be an example yourself of a healthy, happy LGBTQ adult. And yes, you'll also have romantic love. You will have a long, beautiful relationship with someone named Jeff. It will surprise you, teach you a ton of new things, and inspire the most challenging self-compassion work of your life. Your yearning for romance will fold into a more profound love than you have ever known.

You will be keenly aware that not everybody needs or even wants romantic love, but you will treasure your husband (yes, husband!) who you'll get married to on a computer during a pandemic. But that's another story! You'll treasure your husband so profoundly, and you will cherish the family that you will build together. I have another surprise for you. The family you've yearned for your whole life—the family that you imagine you can create when you go away to college and finally come out—that family comes true most beautifully and profoundly later in your life. Person by person, connection by connection, we will build the family we never got in our young life. We will take the reins and create a new circle of love. We'll give up trying to have our life together so that people will like us. Instead, we'll start connecting over the flowing unpredictability of life. We'll also begin connecting over the shared pain of what life can be sometimes. We will build a family because although you have had a painful life up until now, we are not alone.

Lots of people have experienced what you've experienced. Some because they're LGBTQ, and some for other reasons. Let's just say there are a lot of bad parents out there. I love you so profoundly. I know that you think you don't know what's next or what to do, but you, at eighteen, may be the surest we ever are in our entire life. You understand the human heart. You know what bullies are and why they do what they do. And you understand why abuse happens. You know all you want for your life instead of abuse.

I am so proud of you. You came out. You built a life of integrity and honesty, and you are going off to college, a grand adventure in the big city. Despite everything that has happened to you and everything you have been through, you are still full of hope. Even today I draw strength from your hope. Thank you, Jeffrey. Please don't ever change.

Write a letter to yourself at age eighteen. Were you rebellious? Bold? Shy, but wishing to break free? What did you want most of all at age eighteen? Did you ever get it? Tell your young self that you love who they are. Tell eighteen-year-old you all the excellent advice possible about going out into the real world. Say with clarity how proud you are of the focus and passion of eighteen-year-old you.

Epilogue

Find the Light

You know everything that you need to know. All the wisdom and the power you need right now is inside of you. Yes, it's great to have friends and to have compatriots. It is a beautiful thing to walk through this life with beautiful people. And please don't forget how beautiful you are. Please don't forget that you give the best advice. But will you take your own advice?

It's time to stop worrying about what other people think of you.

It's time to move on from trying to be a confident person or worrying about whether you'll seem authentic to other people.

It's time to move on from hiding behind not knowing what to do.

It's not that you *always* have clarity about what's going to come next in your life, but there is a lot you do know. And there is a lot you can celebrate about who you are and all the wisdom you've earned.

Now, don't be afraid to act. Don't be scared to take the next step. For you, the next step will look like belonging. The belonging you always wanted when you were a kid, when you were a teen, when you were a young adult, it's all waiting for you. No matter where you are today, the belonging you've always wanted is something you can work on creating right now for yourself and others. So many people I work with and encounter every day won't act because they fear making a mistake, failing, or *being seen as* having made a mistake, or *being seen as* a failure. People fall prey to this fear because they assume that mistakes or being judged will lead to them no longer belonging. If you make a mistake, you'll be judged. If the group judges you, you won't belong. You can work to create your own nonjudgmental spaces.

There is no way to control what other people think of you. What you can work on and what you can change—sometimes quickly, sometimes slowly—is how you feel about yourself. You can reach deep down and change, moment by moment, step by step, the esteem you hold for yourself. Spiritual practice might make you very angry. It's ironic but true! There might be times when the injustice and cruelty of the world will bring you to a boiling point. There may be times when the unfairness you see around you, whether directed at you or someone else, will make you want to rage. That rage is powerful, and it can be a powerful place to start in your quest to end the abuse that is so common in our world. That anger can act as fuel to start you on a journey toward authentic action. Your action will bring about the justice you've always been craving for yourself and the fairness you've always been craving for the world.

As you work toward a *better* world for everyone, you'll probably make some mistakes. You won't be able to get your life together, or keep your life together, or have your life together. There will be times when you'll trip, fall, and be ashamed of things you've done. It's those times that I would ask you to ride life like it's a giant wave on an unpredictable ocean. I would ask you to stay clear about the direction life wants you to go because it may differ from the direction you think you are trying to go. You might even get to the point where you enjoy the unpredictability.

And lastly, I hope you come to see your pain as beautiful. Please don't worry about seeing *what happened to you* as beautiful. Please don't worry about coming to terms with what happened or finding peace with what happened. To put it simply, please find yourself delightful. The fact that you are a compassionate, good, and kind person who is innocent enough that tragedy makes you feel pain is one of the best things about you.

When I was dancing around in the barn as a kid, one of my favorite dresses had a long green skirt. It was high waisted—an empire waist, they call it. The waist fell just from the bottom of my sternum. And above the waist, above the flowing, hunter green, floor-length skirt, was a cream lace top. I think I stole that gown from Mom, and it was a bridesmaid outfit she wore for one of her friends. I don't know if she ever missed that dress, but I gave it a perfect home. I loved it. I gave it a new place of honor in the black trunk with gold hardware that I hid in the barn behind some hay bales. When I would twirl in my cream top and green-skirted gown, wearing long white gloves that I found at a thrift store, the dust from the bales of hay would kick up from the floorboards and float through each slat of light. The barn walls were planks, and as the light streamed in, it lit those specks of dust. And I would get a little dizzy from spinning. I would get a little happy. And a little free.

We can't control what life brings to us.

We can't control what dust we might kick up.

But I will be forever grateful for that barn.

I will be forever thankful for the Little Jeffrey who created a safe space from nothing so that I could survive long enough to be the integrated, whole, loving, caring, innocent, angry, and full Big Jeffrey that I am today.

Dear Big Jeffrey, Age Forty-Four

You have been through so much. You're middle-aged now, baby! I know you thought you'd never be here. When you were a kid, you thought you wouldn't make it to twenty. And then, when you made it to twenty, you thought you wouldn't make it to thirty. And then, when you made it to thirty, not to forty. And on and on. Now you're forty-four. You have a beautiful husband and a beautiful home. You're married, which you never thought was possible. I remember when you were a kid watching the news, twelve inches from the TV, wide-eyed and eight years old. 1985. A news broadcast about AIDS, what they then called GRID, "gay-related immune deficiency." Rock Hudson had died. The news footage showed his body, covered in a pristine white sheet and on a gurney, being wheeled across a California hill— from above, the news helicopter's blades shook the sheet.

You thought, Well, people like me don't make it. *So you've carried death and life with you always. I hope you're proud to be forty-four. I hope you're pleased to be all grown up. I also know that when you were a kid, you never once thought about getting married. You felt like that was only for straight people. Only for "normal" people, and besides, you never dreamed you'd find someone who would love you enough to marry you. But now, through luck or fate, Jeff is in your life.*

Someone who's non-abusive! Someone communicative! Someone kind! Someone full of life who helps you live! Yes, it's true, not everybody needs a romantic partner. Yes, it's true; there's no way to earn or do more work to find a romantic partner. But if I could give you one important message, it would be this: Enjoy your time with Jeff. Love on him more, with more tremendous enthusiasm, and with as little shame as possible. Say the words I love you more. Spend time together and enjoy each other.

I'd also like to make a request. Please spend time with me. Please spend time with all of us, all the sides of you, all the times of you. Let's take the inner kids out for a playdate and keep our focus on what matters most in life. There are many distractions and many people who would hope to pull you away from your mission. But in the future, I know how important your mission is. I know how unimportant haters, detractors, and people who make snide comments on the internet are.

I know that the work you already do has changed and saved lives. First of all, your life has been saved by the work you do. But I also know that you don't talk much about the positive emails you get every day. You don't talk about what the emails say. "Your video saved my life." It's okay to pause and take in how important that is. As a traumatized kid who's now an adult (who still carries some of that trauma), you'll often want to gloss over what you've accomplished. Please don't. You've already changed the world, and I'm incredibly grateful for you. Let's keep in touch. I love you.

Acknowledgments

I first need to thank Bea Arthur. That may sound odd, but I would not have survived my young life without this quick-witted and brilliant actress. Bea defied gender stereotypes as a deep-voiced, assertive woman. And she often played characters that hit close to home for me: unloved, awkward around men, but self-assured and intelligent. It didn't hurt my fandom that her *Golden Girls* character, Dorothy, had built a relationship with her mother based on sarcasm and being mocked. No wonder I was *Golden Girls*–obsessed. Thank you, Bea.

My beloved editor, Lauren Appleton, has made me a much better writer. I can't thank her enough for her kind and wise guidance. She was also the first to see the value in *Take Your Own Advice*, and on many levels, this book would not exist without her.

Nicolas Newburn has been a delightful and steadfast assistant during the writing of this book. I could not ask for a more astute and understanding helper, reader, and friend.

A special thank-you is owed to Alison Becker and

Patty Jausoro. Both Patty and Alison have been great friends and encouraging colleagues during the creation of this book. I am lucky to have such good people in my life, who constantly help me see the best in me.

There are many trans, nonbinary, and LGBTQ people who have filled my life with delight and inspiration. I am everything I am because of Laverne Cox, Billy Porter, Jonathan Van Ness, ALOK, Dylan Mulvaney, Jacob Tobia, Zach Barack, Rosie O'Donnell, Demi Lovato, Michaela Jaé Rodriguez, Halsey, Tegan and Sara, and Indya Moore. Alexandra Billings and Angelica Ross are deeply inspirational actors and beautiful people. I will always love and respect Janet Mock, Peppermint, Elliot Page, Trixie and Katya, and Jazz Jennings. Chris Mosier and Asia Kate Dillon are trailblazing inspirations. Eddie Izzard helps me to see humor and kindness in dark times. Throughout my life, a few historic trans people's stories have captivated and sustained me. Marsha P. Johnson and Sylvia Rivera inspire great reverence in me, as do Barbette (the drag performer), Julian Eltinge, and Christine Jorgensen. Lili Elbe's life history transformed my early understanding of how to be LGBTQ.

And to the love of my life, Jeff, I owe everything. I could only see myself as worthy through his eyes. He never needs me to be perfect. His patience in holding my hand while I have remembered, discovered, and told my story has saved my life.

Further Reading

Modern HERstory by Blair Imani is an inspirational portrait of the bravest women and nonbinary people throughout recent history. Blair's flair for historical narrative is unmatched. She is brilliant and her enthusiasm for giving voice to the voiceless is crystal clear.

This Time for Me by Alexandra Billings is hands down the best trans memoir I have ever read. Alexandra is inspirational herself, but she is also so raw and revealing and uplifting.

There Is Nothing Wrong with You by Cheri Huber is where I began my spiritual journey. The title says it all, and every page of this great book rings true today.

The Wisdom of Insecurity by Alan Watts. It's okay not to know! Alan walks us through the spiritual foundations of Zen Buddhism with an emphasis on honoring our insecurities.

So You Want to Talk About Race by Ijeoma Oluo. I have followed Ijeoma on social media for years. Her kind wit and no-nonsense style shine through in this guidebook for everyone who cares about racial justice and creating a more equitable world.

Adult Children of Emotionally Immature Parents by Lindsay C. Gibson is the book for you if you suspect that you may have had some childhood trauma. Lindsay's book set off many alarm bells in my head, and I recall having several aha moments wondering how she knew so much about me.

Bird by Bird by Anne Lamott is a vital book for any writer. Anne walks you through opening your heart and mind onto the page. And she details how to keep writing fulfilling and fun.

Dolly Parton's *Dream More* (go ahead, buy the deluxe version) will open your mind to new levels of self-kindness, and Dolly will inspire you to expand your dreams. Through charming stories and solid advice, Dolly breaks down how to see yourself as someone who deserves to dream *more*, not less.

The Happiness Curve by Jonathan Rauch. I'm forty-four at the writing of this book, and I had no idea that I was approaching the bottom of the Happiness Curve. This eye-opening book synthesizes the latest research about the "slump" many of us feel in midlife and how we can beat the crisis and enjoy our middle years.

Set Boundaries, Find Peace by Nedra Glover Tawwab is a personal favorite. Most talk around boundaries gets into self-hate territory very quickly. It's easy to blame the victim (ourselves) for having "weak boundaries." But Nedra gives practical and profound context that can help anyone make a change.

Sissy by Jacob Tobia is both poetically heart-opening and politically astute. Sissy is a must-read for anyone who grew up as an outsider.

About the Author

Jeffrey Marsh's TikToks and compassionate short-form videos have over one billion views. Jeffrey is a viral TikTok and Instagram star, nonbinary activist, and LGBTQ keynote speaker. Jeffrey was the first nonbinary public figure to appear on national television, being interviewed on Newsmax in 2016, and Jeffrey was the first celebrity activist to use they/them pronouns. Jeffrey's #1 bestseller, *How to Be You*, was the first nonbinary memoir. And Jeffrey is the first nonbinary author to sign a book deal with any "Big Five" publisher worldwide, with Penguin Random House. *How to Be You* topped Oprah's Gratitude Meter and was named Excellent Book of the Year by TED-Ed.

Jeffrey's category-nonconforming book, *How to Be You*, ushered in a new literary genre, melding three previous and popular book formats. The book is part memoir, part Buddhist advice, and part workbook. With soaring, direct, and above all, kind prose, *How to Be You* lays out the steps to end self-hate in this lifetime. Jeffrey no longer lives with self-hate, and their memoir tells you how you can break free from self-hate too. *How to Be You* has been so popular and acclaimed that Barnes & Noble rereleased it as a proprietary edition—a rare event for any book, especially one less than five years old. *How to Be You* has been popular throughout the world, with bestselling editions published in regions ranging from the UK to Vietnam. And *How to Be You* also received the rare honor of being a bestseller in both print and audio (voiced by Jeffrey).

Jeffrey is currently America's most in-demand non-binary public speaker, with a mega-viral TED talk. Jeffrey has spoken at the UN and for global brands like Target and BNP. Jeffrey is the world's foremost commentator on non-binary identity and trans activism. Jeffrey is the only non-binary activist to be targeted directly on Tucker Carlson's Fox News program in prime time. *Rolling Stone* recently detailed the hate Jeffrey has received from the far right in America and profiled the strength of Jeffrey's ability to fight hate with love. Jeffrey has reported on LGBTQ topics for *Good Morning America*, *The New York Times*, *Variety*, *TIME*, and the BBC. In addition, Jeffrey was an LGBTQ consultant for Elizabeth Warren's presidential campaign and has consulted for New York University, GLAAD, MTV, Condé Nast's *Them*, and *Teen Vogue*.

Jeffrey has studied and taught Zen for over twenty years. Their rigorous training while living as a monk at a Buddhist monastery in California (as chronicled in *How to Be You*) resulted in Jeffrey receiving the status of pre-cepted facilitator in the Soto Zen tradition of Buddhism.

The rank of precepted facilitator is an elite category and marks a Zen practitioner trained to assist anyone toward spiritual growth. Jeffrey is a highly sought-after break-through and gender counseling coach, helping straight and LGBTQ people attain a lasting sense of peace and self-compassion. Jeffrey regularly coaches celebrities, CEOs, and politicians, helping clients achieve real results and sustainable change.

also by jeffrey marsh

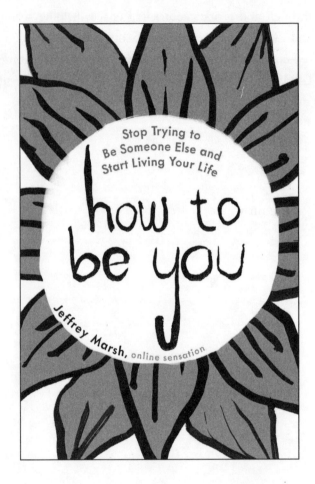

Stop Trying to
Be Someone Else and
Start Living Your Life

how to
be you

Jeffrey Marsh, online sensation

tarcherperigee